OLIVER TYSON

Godology

Copyright © 2025 by Oliver Tyson

First edition

*This book was professionally typeset on Reedsy.
Find out more at reedsy.com*

Contents

I On God

1. Who Is God?   3
2. Where Is God?   9
3. Why Is God?   15
4. When Is God?   19
5. What Is God?   24

II World

6. Worlds   31
7. Worlds Within Worlds   38
8. Heaven and the Higher Worlds   42
9. Destroying Worlds   49
10. Attaining Higher Worlds   54

III Love

11. God Is Love   61
12. Leaf, Sun, Primordial Singularity   67
13. Gravity, Romance, and Quantum Entanglement   73
14. On the Cosmic Horrors   79
15. Key and King   85

IV Life

16	Chapter Sixteen	93
17	The Great Work	99
18	The Pilgrim's Path	104
19	A Touch of Necromancy	109
20	And Burn It with Fire	115

V Conclusion

21	New Eyes	123
22	The Gospel	131

I

On God

1

Who Is God?

As a friend who always has time to listen, or for a phone call. Like that person who has little to no ability to help at the moment and gives that little bit of encouragement. Those few words that kept the energy up at key moments or kept the work going. Or even as that person, stranger even, who agrees, at the market or store, or some public place. One who agrees that some third party was out of line to say what they said or do what they did. The idea of God is stretched over our lives as thinly as our understanding of him.

We could say that we meet God in a sermon, a static being, an unapproachable entity. Omnipotent, omniscient, omnipresent. Distant, usually, and almost lifeless. It may be here that we hear about him, but a true experience is a thing that comes from a different source. Time and church only drill in facts, like nails. A correspondence in word only, like being told of a story, of a painting, of a place one wants to see. God is like a mountain, a completely different experience for everyone. From those who merely love his shade over their homes in the early evening. To those who fall short of the ability to climb his skirt. To those who are well trained and find no challenge in reaching his top. Even those who are so busy with their hobbies, works, and lives, that they don't even notice its presence. Some are raised, climbing up and down as children. Making it an integral part of their lives, even deep into adulthood. At the same time, some put it aside, as with all other childish things. Some grew up in a flat land and so have a fresh, childish wonder upon looking up at the peak. And then there are those born, live, and die on a flat land. Never having a single thought about anything more than the rising rim of a gopher hole.

Within the halls of any place of worship, one will hear many times the soliloquy of a Testimony. A story of one individual's introduction to this character. In these stories, one finds this character to be the staunchest supporter and the truest friend. The strongest defender, the softest mother, the wisest teacher, and sometimes, just that one who never gave up and was always there. And it usually is followed by some kind of call to some kind of altar. An invitation to those particular listeners who asked one particular question: who is God? Not a static, unknowable all-seeing ever-present distant watcher. But a character of meaning, capable of bonding, capable of friendship. A character dependable and, most importantly, forgiving.

God cannot be explained; the only word that can bring us any semblance of understanding is "infinite." There is nothing else about God or about his essence that can be known. With the singular exception, as every believer will confirm, what he says of himself. God is said to speak through one book or many. Through the universe itself or as a whisper heard only within a point in the heart. He chooses the time and place, and he chooses what is communicated. But it only takes one true Testimony to light a fire in the heart of nearly anyone witnessing. However, sometimes, even a life of searching fails to compare to that one presentation, of that one witness to the "greatness" of this character, that one time. Some commit to one church, belief, or community, finding some sense of peace, and what can only be described as a relationship of some sort with something higher than the sum of its parts. Elusive but explainable under the moniker God.

Others go far and wide to the most obscure beliefs and those most esoteric of thoughts and practices. And some of this kind find an essence as well. A thing that exists and whose existence cannot be questioned. But what it is, defined, is as before, elusive. It is felt; that is irrefutable. They feel something, but what is it? It feels in some ways like a full stomach, like satiation. In other ways, it feels like the resonance of proximity to loved ones. Sometimes, it feels like a call to adventure that a good movie may inspire. And in yet other ways, it feels quite the opposite, like hunger or distance. At times, it feels almost sinful. Is this that Infinite God? Is it related? And if not, is it proof of the presence or nearness of it?

God cannot be explained. Even the feeling of him lies just beyond our vocabulary. But that doesn't mean that silence is an option when felt. How does one explain the draw, that force that will take someone across the whole world, looking for a feeling that cannot be described, explained, or even understood? How does one describe to another a mere vision of heaven? Especially when that heaven is a place that they have never actually grasped. They have felt it, but they have never been. It is truly the highlight of life. An experience that one would want to share with the world, just by the slightest passing of the presence, just by the merest touch of the feeling.

But a feeling is all it is, lacking the words to define or express what it was that was felt. And there is a reason for this. A word comes up every time one tries to explain. A word that ruins the entire explanation, reduces the entire experience, and reeks of sin and ignorance : "Just."

A delicious donut is "just" some flour and a bit of sugar.

A trip to Disney Land with friends is "just" a long, expensive walk, and waiting in lines.

A lover's kiss, "just" a wet smack.

"Just" can, and usually is, followed by "nothing more." The ultimate mood killer. "Nothing More" takes from the experience all of the existence that overlayed the static facts of the experience, as if they didn't matter, or hold substance. But no, the experience must exist on a higher level than the physical, and so it is so much more. There is more felt than this corporal reality. And sometimes, when there is some gradience of "darkness to light"; sometimes, when we foray into this deeper, or higher, existence, often due to hardships and sufferings, or even greater splendors and pleasures; sometimes, a presence is felt, unknown and unknowable. Unrecognizable, only as something new that has never been seen or felt before. And in so many places, and in so many experiences, that thing, in that place, higher reality, or plane of existence, is called God. God is, and resides within, what can only be called heaven. And if one can believe these tellers of the Testimonies, then this God, once felt, is relatable, companionable.

God cannot be explained. But to those who have a relationship with him, there is almost nothing else to talk about. There is no topic more personal, no place more intimate. And no dreams are separate. To the outsider listening to an impassioned Testimony, there is a resounding question, more felt than asked. What is this force within this person? What is this light? Also known as, who is God? A question that receives no lack of answers, but every answer speaks to that old static being of infinite proportions that is unapproachable and emotionally distant.

But to the question of who is God? That character who saves and loves. A live, live in partner in life. A real friend. The answers are as elusive as the feeling itself, or they are about his other, static persona as if a different being entirely. One can take solace in the idea that the journey is more important than the destination or that God will meet them when it's time. These answers help to soothe the anguish caused by looking for that thing that some other person has. The balm is not a cure. But a cure exists; it is a different understanding or a hidden wisdom.

What is actually meant when it is said that God will meet you in his time? Or even that God works in mysterious ways? These avoidances and evasions can be understood as attempts to steer clear of the sin of the word "just." An attempt to say something without diminishing the feeling, the true dimension of the experience. God is infinite, and so, it is with our finite senses that we experience him. He doesn't change; only our eyes adjust. It is like taking in the entire ocean into a small vessel. A cup or some Tupperware. We bring a bowl to hold the ocean and feel a deep despair when unsuccessful.

And because God is infinite, this cannot be described as a failure on any part as we have to attempt to fit the ocean inside our little bowls to have any sense of the Infinite at all. Like a blind man rubbing his hands on the side of a building, increasing his understanding of bricks a thousandfold. This is not failure; instead, it is completely by design, being both righteous and godly.

Another way of seeing this dilemma, as opposed to the ocean in a cup, is as assumptions and presumptions that an Infinite God must be fully aware of the limitations of others. Note our many "assumptions" of the Infinite God; this is merely where we are in our journey. To honestly seek the source of the Testimonies and the root of the experiences that seem to transcend the natural.

We are embarked on a journey that creates within us an understanding or a true desire for the answer. God begins within us a block of static information. And within it is planted a seed through hearing a fervent Testimony. It grows almost like a weed, and this weed is the evolution of the question.

"Who is God?" This question is like a child playing in the water with a small bowl. Asking for infinite knowledge to fill our small (in comparison) minds. We slowly (and sometimes painfully) grow to ask a question of bite-sized proportions. Not the entire ocean, but just a cupful of the waters. We ask for the bit of the answer that we are capable of grasping. But the answers expand our minds to ask more directly: "Who is God to you?"

2

Where Is God?

Who is God to me? Or what of the infinite can I begin to chew on? After all, that is how any form of relationship begins. If we accept the Testimonies of the witnesses and the teachings of books, then God, as an infinite being, does not and cannot fit into our bowl, which is the entire point of the question "Who is God?" Now, we understand this new question, and ask it honestly. But when we ask, "Who is God to me?" why is it not immediately answered?

It is now understandable that before, we received no reply from above. The question was impossible to answer, as no aspect of the infinite is less than infinite. But if both parties, God and man (assuming from the Testimonies), seek each other, with the understanding that they can only meet in the small mind of the mortal being, nothing should stand in the way. And an experience should transpire directly.

But it is in silence that we are left, asking if this infinite being, whose presence we accept purely within faith, even wants anything to do with us at all. And we begin to compare ourselves with those who gave the Testimonies in the first place.

"They were good enough, so why aren't I?" Not to judge, but some of those people were real pieces of work. And if God met them, befriended them, rescued them, and remained with them, then what did we miss? And we begin to ask then, "Where is God?" And we ask this in the material sense, substantially. Where is God locally that I may go and find him?

We may begin and do something stupid, like go to the actual place where some other person had gone and had their experience. Go where they went and do what they did. We could attempt to duplicate someone else's experience, but all to no avail. We can understand this, usually even before we go, as it is the experience that we seek, not the activities. Someone can tell us that they had the greatest time at the theater, and another may question them, saying, "I've been to that theater and did not have anything close to what you've described." This does not make the initial a liar; it was a different affair. A different crowd, different food, perhaps even a different movie. The same way that eating a danish is more about the "eating" than the "danish." After returning from abroad or from wherever. We return with the same questions as we left and with no answers to them. But we will find that the questions have turned.

"Where is God?" means nothing if he is hiding. So then, where is he, not in the material sense? But where are his thoughts? Maybe he was looking for us and just missed us? Looked over or looked past. We are quite small, so this is understandable. Maybe God is looking for something more, as some of the Testimonies included stories of copious drug use and tantamount danger. World travel and violence. Maybe God is looking for more. So where is he looking, and what is he looking for? How does one become worthy of an audience with a king?

First, we asked "Who is God?" And then it was, "Who is God to me?" But if we look high and low, in and out, and no life-changing encounter with this character has befallen us, then who am I to God? And what if what I am is not what he is looking for? The difference could be that not only are we incapable of fitting all the Infinity of this character into our bowls, but that we even have the audacity to try.

It is as if we called on a king to halt the business and affairs of his kingdom, cancel his plans and all meetings, and rush forthwith to our table. To break bread with us and tell us all about himself. It would be arrogant for the greatest among the people, much more so for us. In this way, it is obvious that we are microbial to God and should not ask to draw him down to us. But to humbly lift us up to him. And this is kind of our only choice.

We can build on this assumption. If God is infinite and has proven through Testimony that he is known, and knowable to his followers and believers, knowable even to the point of friendship, then we can believe that not only must he know of us, but he must know of the absence, the place within us that we feel for him to fill. He must know and have known. He must have known even before we knew, even before we were. He knew and was capable of establishing himself within us. Can knowledge and opportunity be enough to convict on the charge of intent?

God can be convicted, so much so that even the "God" within our desires is merely a placement, an Avatar of his design. This God is the creator, source, and beginner of even our search for him. All knowing and all being. Who are we to him? Who are we that he would place a desire within us and then go run and hide? When we search for him in all the places, we find more and more where he isn't. Perhaps and mayhaps, if we search for ourselves, we will draw closer and closer to where he is.

This may sound like quite the egoistic position, but that is only because we see ourselves as somehow outside of reality, observing it. Or that we see God, outside of reality, controlling it. We are looking for our answers within God. God knows this, yet remains hidden. These two assumptions combined lead to the conclusion that maybe God wants us to look elsewhere and for something else entirely. This elsewhere search can be called looking for ourselves.

Ourselves in a different light, as in our depths. What makes us, drives us, compels us. Not to look in a mirror and find our noses. But look out into the endless worlds and find, with our noses, even the faintest scent of our calling. Our drive and purpose. This is what we mean by "Who am I to God?" Within it is, why do I even look? Why do I believe in the sermons or the Testimonies? Why am I driven to care? Where is the origin of the drive? And who is in control of the journey? Is God a component of my world or am I a component of his?

For example, say a very talented person builds a car, creating it from scratch, from the metal to the wiring to the plastic to the rubber. Every component is created with care and with love. Upon completion, when his work is done, the front left tire pops off. The tire rolls off into the distance, looking for adventure, looking for purpose, looking for the one who created it.

Who am I to God? To explain this question, to really delve into it, ask, "Who am I in God's world? In God's eyes?" Or, more simply, since God is eternal and infinite, the real question is, "Who am I?"

What separates us, in our desires toward this character, from others? Like the mountain metaphor before, some are content with a simple shade or a nightly jaunt up the slope. Some enjoy a hard climb, while others love its mere existence on the horizon. God pulls some to challenge him and pulls others to enjoy his presence. Each has their own relationship with him. Humans are social creatures and have an intrinsic need for chumming up with others. Where there has been a lack of this aspect of life, the relief can feel stronger than the sum of its parts, leading to what we might call a religious experience. But there is no way to quantify the feeling or even to compare and contrast. What is community for one person may have tinges of God for another, as the feeling of God exists in the same realm as the produce (yields/profits) of community. As with nature, when walking through a forest, a palpable feel is present that is not tree or leafy in any way. But this feeling can be related to the soothing of depression and the reception of fresh air.

These feelings are a part of life, just as the road or harsh wind to a tire. God or Godless? Finite or infinite? Where does the feeling of a character end, and the feelings of life created by this character begin? A long way of saying that maybe God doesn't want us to find him, and perhaps it is delusional to think that he does. Delusional to see ourselves as somehow outside of his design. Perhaps what God wants for us is to just be part of his plan as he planned it in the first place. Just like the tire accepts its place on the wheel, the car won't work without the tire, and maybe the world won't work without you.

The grander question arises from this tire answer and is probably the biggest question yet. If God is the creator and created the heavens and the Earth, as the witnesses claim, than why did he make us in a way that we would leave everything behind and go looking for him? And even for those of us who didn't go looking for some otherworldly essence or being, some character from outside our dimension, the energy and thoughts devoted to him, even from within or lives and purposes, surely could have been better spent. In other words, tires don't pop off and go searching; they fulfill their purpose entirely, without awareness that they are even doing it. The question asked here is, are we doing the same thing? Fulfilling our purpose without even the awareness of it by endlessly seeking some answer to some question that we can't even articulate? We ask ourselves: What is the meaning of my life? Where do I belong? And why am I here? The tire acts as it is intended to act. What if we do the same?

The question "Who am I?" can be asked in yet another way. Or from another angle. Why am I questioning? Why am I seeking? Why am I not enough? Why is God doing this to me? Why is God even a thing? Why did God introduce himself in his own creation? Why would an author write himself into his own story? All of these, or simply: "Why is God?"

3

Why Is God?

Why is God? And why would an author write himself into his own story? Not to mention, he caused the characters in his story to chase him in some kind of grand game of tag in which one of the players (God) has given himself the greatest portion of the hiding expertise. Where did this story of his even begin? And who is he in his own words?

Why is God? In our books, his story begins with the creation of the world, forming man from clay and breath. The man was placed in a garden to name all the plants and animals, plucking a rib out of his body and fashioning it into a woman. God promptly kicked them out of the place where he had placed them due to disobedience. This is a story heard many times over a religious upbringing. And often in daily life, as it is such a popular tale. This story introduces many of the incongruities known in all writings of God. God makes mistakes here when creating the man alone and having to put him back under to finish the job. He is physical when he walks through the gardens. And there seem to be things that he does not know, to which he must ask, which is not accurate to the term omniscient. The God presented here appears different from every other story in which we find God. Even the modern idea of God is never reduced as far as in this story. Still, this story is heard many times during a religious upbringing and often in daily life. Nearly everyone has heard it in some fashion.

But there is another story, drowned in history, that very few people ever hear. A story of a man named Adam. Adam was a man born approximately six thousand years ago, shy by a few hundred or so. He was not the first man to be born but was destined to be called the first man due to a singular thought in his mind. Adam was of the priestly class, meaning that he was more of a thinker. In those days, working, fighting, and thinking were the main functions of society. His job was to help those who were less of the thinkers to survive.

One day, while taking a break from his occupational thoughts, he was sitting outside, on a rock, looking (not directly) at the sun. And here on this rock, Adam had a thought. Adam thought that everything that he saw, every bird, beast, and animal, even every creeping thing that crawled on the face of the Earth, every plant, flower, and tree, in time and at its time, ended. Everything had a birth, a life, and a death. Life itself is just the name of the space between the other two, birth and death. A beginning and end, a cause and an effect. But more than that, Adam saw that the effect of one often was the cause of another. Everything was a cause of an effect, and an effect of some cause. And every cause had its creator (cause). He looked at the sun and wondered if it, too, had a creator. As it was also, like every other thing that existed, a thing that existed, he assumed that it did also have a cause for its existence. He also assumed that if everything lived and died, everything had a cause, a creator.

Then, at some point in the past, there had to be a cause of all causes, a beginning of everything. And he began to think of what that thing could be. He had many, many thoughts about this one thing. But only two will be brought here. One was that this thing had to be infinite. Because if it wasn't infinite, then it too would have a beginning, and thus have a thing that began it (a cause). And that cause, whatever it was, would be another link in a chain that needed to have an end. Like the number Pi, either having a final number in its calculation or revealing a loop, both possibilities being an end. In the same way, the cycle of cause and effect must have an end, even a form of infinite looping would consist of an end, cause of all causes.

This thing, of which he was thinking, had to be the thing, the cause of all causes. And the thing, had to be infinite. Second, this thing was one solid thing, not two things close together. If this thing were two things, then that little empty place between the two things, the separateness, would also be a thing. And so then there would be three things. So this thing had to be one thing, that held no relation to any other thing but instead was truly the creator of all the things, and nothing existed before it or around it. These days, we call that thing the Big Bang, but Adam didn't know that. He just called this thing The Infinite. Adam devoted his life to the study of this Infinite thing and made many discoveries.

One massive discovery that he made was that if everything that existed was caused and created by this Infinite thing, then that would include all things, even those things that we didn't think of as things at all, like thoughts themselves. Thus, Adam discovered a whole other world. The world of mind and of thoughts. A world built of thought, as this world is built of matter. And he discovered that this world was just like the was living in and the rock he was sitting on. It was ...... by the infinite thing that created the world he was living in and the rock he was sitting on. Then he wondered: if his own thoughts were shaped by the being that created all thoughts through the same chain of cause and effect as the material world, then his thoughts about the Infinite must also have come from the Infinite itself. And that was just too much to be a coincidence. Here, he realized that even though he had discovered the Infinite, the Infinite new him and had known him from the beginning. Adam had an experience with this character and had a Testimony to tell. He told his Testimony to many people, even calling them to study with him, this Infinite thing. His Testimony has been passed down (altered though it was) throughout the ages to this day.

Adam was led to the Infinite. He understood himself, not as a corporeal being with a body and a will, but as an incorporeal idea, an Infinite Endless inevitability. There was nothing that he knew about the personhood of this being, only of its existence. His study spawned from his own understandings, thoughts, and desires concerning this being. Thoughts and desires that only existed because of the cause-and-effect nature of this being. And through the process of anthropomorphization of the Infinite, God was.

It was sitting on a rock, thinking about things, both beginnings and ends, that led Adam to an encounter with the Infinite. And it can be that the Infinite is still there.

4

When Is God?

At the end of the last chapter, we left with the supposition that Adam was led to the Infinite. But in our understanding of this Infinite, it does not act with any will as an intelligent being. Naturally, our use of the word "intelligent" implies our own. Intelligence means a comparison to that of enlightened mankind; anything too far above us is an act of nature. Anything above us is too high for us to recognize. In this way, the Infinite is not intelligent based on our understanding. To compare this Infinite to the character that we are introduced to in our time appears as a different being altogether.

We ended with the idea to go back and copy Adam's method of communing with Infinite, which is to ask the question, "When is God?"

"When is God?" is an odd question (grammatically) to ask, but it is an important one. The quintessential aspects of God, from Adam's contemplation, have seemingly been forgotten in time. If he is eternal, omnipresent, omniscient, and omnipotent, as we are told, this begs the question: why does he so often change?

Why does God change as with the time and seasons? Why is his book so full of reactions? God likes or loves. He dislikes and hates and is full of displeasure. He judges and questions and sometimes even changes his mind. Why is God so dramatic at one time and so uncaring in others?

How did God go from Adam's Infinite thing to an innocuous being, static and distant? These answers are found not in the Infinite but in the other world that Adam discovered. The world of the mind is a world built on thought, just as ours is built on matter. Adam discovered many discernments about this world, three of which will be discussed here. In this other world, space and time do not exist. And we can find this in our own exploration of this other world.

First, on space, as in physical location, here and there.

Imagine we were standing in a group, and one says:

"I am thinking of a kind of bird."

One of of the others in the group guesses, "Is it a dove?"

The first says "No."

(To help with the analogy, the answer is a Raven.)

The second asks, "Was I close?"

And the first replies, "Not remotely."

A different person asks, "Is it a Bluebird?"

And the first replies, "Closer."

Another person in the group stands directly to the left of the first but perhaps does not pay complete attention to the discussion guesses.

"A potato!"

And the first says, "You could not be further away; you are on a different planet!"

This person, however, was not actually standing far away at all; he was directly beside him. We use this terminology all the time. Enough that there is no need to explain how, during the conversation in the group, this person was a million miles away, escaped in his own thoughts.

In our words, we are not talking about location in this corporeal plane. But in the spiritual plane, the world of the mind.

Someone sitting on a bench, overhearing the conversation, calls out, "Is it a crow?"

And the first, still reeling from the outrageous potato, says, "Exactly! Correct! We are of the same mind."

Same mind, same location, as one. Even though the person is on a relatively far park bench. And yes, we are slightly beating a dead horse with this analogy. But here we move on to the next analogy: that of a penguin.

There is no time in the Spiritual Dimension. To understand this, we will picture a penguin. Envision in your mind, visualize, if you will, a penguin. Picture him as clearly as possible; see his fancy dress and his flappy feet. See the little yellow strip on his face, see his black beak, his black, glassy eyes, all of him. And that's it. That is the entire exercise.

Let this image of the penguin pass on and let your mind go elsewhere.

And then we are going to wait minuets, days, even years. And later in life, we will think back upon that old penguin we once contemplated. And we will see that this penguin did not age, did not change. We can test this with other memories as well. We can remember past pets, dogs, cats, or hamsters. Usually, one can recall them quite clearly. And in memory, they exist without time. Not to be unsavory, but we don't remember our first pets as they are now. Buried. When we think about our old pets, the mind goes back in time, to play with them in their prime, at the height of the relationship. And there, our pets will remain, for as long as we live, without time. And even if we move away, and live far away and live in far-off lands, our pets will remain with us, beyond space in any location, and untouchable by time.

These are two aspects that Adam discovered about his other world, which he called the Spiritual Dimension. Now, there is one more discernment that Adam had about his other world that we will dissect here. The ability of a spiritual object to change.

If we go back to our old penguin, that we discussed years ago, we will find it in exactly the same place and way that it was when we left. This penguin is a spiritual object. If we were to take a top hat and place it gently on the penguin's head, we would now have a penguin in a top hat. And that's it. That is the end of our meditation on the penguin.

But not of the penguin in a top hat. The penguin in a top hat is a spiritual object. If we think back, as we did before, as to our first pets in the prime of their life, we can find in our minds (that is, in our spiritual worlds) that the penguin is still there, pre-top hat. This spiritual object, the penguin (no top hat), exists just as any other without time or space. This is an eternal penguin, unchanging in our minds.

Adam discovered that once a spiritual object exists, it exists forever, unvarying. Our penguin in a top hat is a separate object completely. Now, in our minds, two spiritual objects exist; the penguin and the penguin in a top hat. Each stands stoically, unmoving, forever. However, both objects have a relationship to each other, even though both are thought by a thinking mind. The penguin is the cause, while the penguin in a top hat is the effect, as there would be no penguin to put a top hat on if it were not for the eternal penguin that came before. Even in the same way, sitting with God in a top hat, who is ever changing his mind and ignoring us completely at times, We can go back (instead of cause and effect, think effect and its cause) and find a pre-top hatted God, otherwise known as the Infinite.

To clarify, God in a top hat is the character we were introduced to at the beginning. He is the one told to us through the Testimonies we've heard. God in a top hat is the Avatar that we receive by the cascade of causes and effects from the very first existences by the Infinite itself. The Infinite is the mind from which both God and God in a top hat emerged. God in a top hat is the embodied will of the Infinite to draw us to itself. It is, in an anthropomorphic way, intentional.

5

What Is God?

Intentional is the word chosen to end the previous chapter, the intentional will of the Infinite, of the universe, and of many other names. We begin with God by the will of the Infinite. By the pre-initial cause of the entire cascade of causes and effects leading from the beginning. From the beginning of all things, to the beginning of our journey toward the beginning of all things. It is the Infinite that brings us to question who he is through the introduction of the idea and the revealing of the Testimonies. The seed planted within us by the Infinite takes root, and by the Infinite, it blossoms into all manner of questions, each one with its specific root (cause) and each with its particular effect. The question "Who is he?" leading through "Who is he to us?" unto "Who are we to him?" is a cascade designed ultimately by the very him of whom we are asking. A creator, creating a being, and drawing it back to itself, all in one movement.

All of this stems from the mere idea of an Infinite cause of all causes by a man on a stump. As we can see, it is very easy to get ahead of ourselves and of our understanding. We can see from the previous paragraph how this being can grow. This character can grow even further to have an identity outside of what we know and assume from its cascading cause-and-effect nature. This change, from Infinite Endless to Living God, is done by anthropomorphizing the Infinite.

Anthropomorphism is the attribution of human characteristics to an object. And we can attempt to explain this with the example of fire. We can study fire by playing with it, watching it burn and blow away. However, in order to discuss it, we must ask questions that will guide our research. We can anthropomorphize. We ask questions about fire.

"Where are its legs?" How does it move?

"What are its hands?" As in, what does it do?

"What is its stomach?" can mean what does it eat and how does it propagate itself?

"Where is its butt?" could be where does it end, or even how does it relieve itself of its used food?

By trying to understand it, through the means that we understand ourselves, we can easily learn about it, from its own mouth.

But then we can ask deeper questions about the fire.

"Where is its mind?" What is its purpose? why does it burn?

"Where is its heart?"

And with this tool, the Infinite was divided.

The Infinite does not change and is unknowable. But when anthropomorphized, a character is added to the Infinite, which acts like a mirror, reflecting some kind of reason back. The Infinite, through cause and effect, placed the Avatar (God in a top hat) in our minds. Our reason creates a semblance (Infinite in a top hat) of the Infinite to grab onto. This God answers our questions. He answers them because it is his desire to answer them. Because it is his very will that we ask them. And it is this God that we can ask: Who, Where, Why, When, and What, are you? This is the study of God.

This study is of the Infinite, but it is not the Infinite as it is truly is, infinite and unknowable. However, the study exists; it is formless, and faceless, but it exists nonetheless. This study is where his being forms, and through it, we have an audience with the Anthropomorphic Infinite.

All the while, our knowledge grows of all that exists outside of ourselves and all that exists within. This can be spoken of as "the anthropomorphic draws near to us." Coming closer, as for us to see him with our expanding eyes and minds.

In our spiritual world, he draws nearer and nearer. And we begin to understand that all of this is the blueprint of reality, the plan of the Infinite, and so is inevitable. Just as the penguin in a top hat led us to understand God in a top hat, the Infinite itself comes to us as the inevitable, a cascading of will beyond cause and effect but of pure intent.

Now, to say it in a different way, there is the Infinite, and the Infinite exists because the finite exists. And finite exists only when created (began) by a creator (cause). And because the pendulum of cause and effect is in itself an effect, there must be a cause to the causes, a cause of all causes. This cause is unknown and unknowable. It is causeless; it is not an effect. And all things that are effects, are effects of itself.

Secondly, there is the idea that ideas themselves do not exist outside of all things, without roots in the reality caused by the unknowable. The unknowable caused all the things that were caused, and the realm of the mind was no exception. Keep in mind that these causes are unknown and unknowable (by our abilities), and only the effects of these causes can be measured (again by our abilities).

Thirdly, if the cause of all causes (Infinite) causes the effects of the mind, then all the effects of the mind are caused by this cause, including the effects of the mind concerning this cause. In other words, the Infinite, through cause and effect, created a creation that would seek out its creator. And in anthropomorphic terms, God made man to seek Him. And this force of creation, this will, this pure intent that Adam discovered, he called Love.

II

World

6

Worlds

The study of God is about devoting time and attention to acquiring knowledge of the Infinite. As was mentioned earlier, any portion of Infinity is itself Infinite, and so is entirely out of reach of the finite. This is a barrier that we will never be able to overcome. However, in his studies, Adam found a way to transmute the concepts and understand them. Here we will introduce several of these "transmutations."

Now, we could say that the Infinite Endlessness discovered, was Adam's Infinite. But in reality, it is not. The concept of Infinity that we are discussing is that from any point and toward any direction, after an infinite length, this Infinite will be found. Not another Infinite, and not a different Infinite. There is only one Infinite at the end of any line. This sounds reasonable, but for the finite, it is meaningless. The reason that this is being stated is that when we call this "Adam's Infinite," it is not because there are others; it is, instead, the name, of an unknown, unknowable, and unnameable, spiritual object. And by "spiritual object," we mean, of something that can be thought of or exists in the mind. We can hold the entity of the Infinite in our minds. But we cannot hold its truth. We cannot know it as it truly is, only as a name.

To expand this some more and understand what we mean by "name," let us contemplate the sun. Now, upon reading the word "sun," you have probably visualized the yellow ball in the day-lit sky. Smaller than the tip of your little finger and bright enough to burn the eyes after a few seconds of looking. This is obviously not the true magnitude of the sun. And here we run into our quintessential spiritual problem. It is a spiritual problem and not a corporeal problem because we don't have this problem in the Corporeal Dimension. Physically, we can point with a finger or tool. If there is a fruit on the table of which we have forgotten the name, we can point. Others can tell us, "That is an apple," or "That is an orange." But in the spiritual (the world of the mind), there is no pointing. A thing's name is its only identifier. The word "sun" corporeally is as a finger pointing. One could say "light bulb," and if they were pointing, everyone would know of what they spoke.

However, in the spiritual realm, this is not the case, and we can delve into this idea with the sun. In this example, the word "sun" is the name of the spiritual object of the small light in the bright sky. But perhaps one could say "sol" to speak of the very large object in the blackness of space. This object is massive; it is dark, almost black, and has orange spirals of light on it. This is the spiritual object of the mosaic image from a satellite. It is seen by the eye and understood by the mind. This is (if we remember back to the penguin in a top hat) a completely different spiritual object than the "sun" before. And again, we will go deeper with the name "Helios." This is the sun in all its glory, as it truly sits in space. Now, whereas we "know" the size of the sun, we cannot actually visualize its diameter. We see, in our mind's eye, a big, really big ball of light. It is about the size of a really big beach ball, with the words "really big" underneath it. We cannot visualize the true sun, but this spiritual object "Helios," so named, is closer to the reality of the sun than either "sun" or "sol" that came before. This is how spiritual objects work. To "know" the sun is to learn its names. And with the sun itself, even if we knew the "name" of this true diameter, it would not be the name of itself. Because the sun is more than its size; it is its depth. Its many names are the many layers to peel back in order to know its true self. And these names lead, from our senses of it to its sense of itself. We could call this "the study of the sun." And so it is with the study of God. The Infinite, is but a single of many names of God.

A name is a level (or angle) of knowledge, as a "file/folder" of information in the spirit. The name signifies the level from the outside. Just as you don't think of yourself as your name, but think of your name as a title of yourself. Likewise, a name signifies the level from the outside. But from the inside, it feels like a whole world. And within a world is where the study of God begins.

Our world it has trees and skies and mountains and rivers. And our world is amongst other worlds, like Mars and Venus and Jupiter and Saturn. Now, we will begin by saying the worlds discussed in the study of God are a different kind of world. But in reality, they are not. Instead, we will try to argue that the world we live in is not the planet we are on.

We wish to introduce here, three different terms (transmutations) here: reality, dimension, and world.

Reality is unknowable; it is the light before reaching our eyes, the vibration itself without being translated by our ears.

And matter, away from our tongues. It is what exists as it exists, without sugarcoating or dumbing down. It is the entire equation of gravity's pull, even from the farthest stars. And it is the micro, sub-atomic scale. Reality is truly unknowable.

Dimension is a cut of reality. A bite, a level. Dimension is a spectrum of reality that is separated from reality for us to understand. We can think of the dimensions of our visual or auditory spectrums. Or our level of existence on this planet and plane. Dimension is a plane of reality.

And in this simple way, we understand this idea of the use of the word World. We understand the meaning behind the phrase "part of my world." Meaning something that I deal with every day. My world is my city, work, and social circles. Places in my world are places that I frequent, places I enjoy to such a degree that if one were to come to this city and ask where one could watch a good cage fight, the answer of, "I don't know, that's not really a part of my world," would be fully understood.

This is my personal world. But this world is more real than the reality in which I reside, so much so that it is this personal world that I reside in and not the dimension of reality. This point is being made because speaking of the concept of worlds is very difficult. One can say there are two worlds because of the separations we see. But in reality, there is only one reality; there are just many layers to it. The worlds are an illusion of perception.

The difficulty here is using the same word with multiple definitions. A world is not reality (even though it does exist within) nor a dimension. A world is a bubble within a dimension. Your world is your city, job, home, and friends. This is your (personal) world, and it exists neither strictly in the Spiritual Dimension nor the Corporeal. It instead sits within both. Worlds exist across dimensions. This is because there are spiritual (mental) aspects to your work and your city that are included in the understanding of them, and there are spiritual aspects of both that are not part of your personal world. But we could also say that we have a "Job World," and a "City World," and a "Social World."

All of these different worlds are part of our personal worlds. Besides all of these worlds, we have one more world, located purely within the Spiritual World, fully in the Spiritual Dimension. This world is the study of God. This world is not our religiosity; it is not a church or spiritual family, as these things are their own worlds. All other worlds overlap and conjoin each other. This is not only because they exist across dimensions but because of their finite focus. Only the study is opposite because it is a purely spiritual object, eternal and unchanging. In this way, the study of God is the very same as the one begun by Adam in his time, as it is from him (by way of cause and effect) that we receive it. This study is also the very same Avatar implanted within us by the will (cause and effect) of the Infinite.

Two things here need to be addressed. One is why and how God is located only in the spiritual world, specifically because our varied faiths are held dear to us and stand quite significantly within all of our different worlds.

This is because the study of God is entirely focused on the Infinite. All else is the cascading cause and effect issuing from it. And not of it, specifically. In other words, consider the salmon.

Imagine a lake, still and serene, the perfect place to be born if one was a fish. And this lake bed sits upstream of some rather harsh rushing waters. The still waters are the destination, but we are as salmon located down the stream beneath, dealing with the rushing waters. The study of God is like the salmon swimming against the current of waters. The destination is at the top, but the travel and everything that needs to be done within the travel (all the wild swimming) has nothing to do with the still lake at the top. The swim upstream has nothing to do with the waters at the destination. In other words, the actions of the salmon in the rushing waters are dissimilar to the actions of the salmon in the lake bed. And they are only necessary to reach the destination. If the salmon loses sight of his goal and allows his actions to be his purpose, he will be turned around in the rushing chaos and find himself swimming frantically. He will not know that he is going in the wrong direction because all that is around him is water, and he doesn't have a compass. It is the destination that guides him, not the swimming.

The focus must be on the Infinite and not the cascading causes that issue from it, even though all that is known of the Infinite is the cascade issued forth.

The second of the two things needing to be addressed is what a world is.

We have explained the definition of a world with many examples. But using them, manipulating them, and expressing our lives and ourselves through them is not knowing what they are.

A world is a perception. Your world is what you know that you know. It is your understanding, your attainment like a bubble in reality. Reality is all that exists, as it exists, and is interconnected as it exists. And dimensions are gradations of reality. Keep in mind that the dimensions are names of the spectrums within reality. So there are dimensions within dimensions, and both above and below. Reality is divided into many dimensions. And a world is a bubble within it all.

We've used this example before; our worlds are our bowls.

They are our perceptions and our understandings of our surroundings. They are our eyes to reality. And like our eyes, they are not reality, only a means to receive it. The worlds are an illusion, or create an illusion, in the same way a bowl creates an illusion of the ocean by being filled with water. We see by our bowls, but the observer can see across the entire dimensions. The observer can see the reality: that our perception understands as worlds within worlds.

7

Worlds Within Worlds

In previous chapters, we've discussed how there is no understanding to be found in the Infinite. As even a part of the Infinite is infinite. Even its names don't amount to its essence, as they are levels of understanding from our perspective and not from God's, making every name finite added to finite. Now, there is a complication here because we will talk as if we are building our study from the top down, as from God's perspective. But this is also just a name, and still from our perspective. Our perspective of God's perspective is still just our perspective. But it is a start. Why is it a start? Because what is happening on the surface of our minds is less important than what is happening beneath the surface. We discussed what it means when we say "world." By itself, it is perception; your world is your perception. But it is not our perception of the entire reality, as the reality is Infinite. As was introduced earlier, there is only one Infinite, and it is the same Infinite. The words reality, universe, all, infinite, source, and endless each refer to the same "object." They just speak of different aspects, angles, or directions of looking at that same object. So, our worlds are not the perception of reality but perception of dimensions. And dimensions are just relatable spectrums within reality that help us communicate a small piece of reality to our understanding. Dimensions are parameters of measurement of the infinite. The word reality is a word that we understand but don't feel. This is why the word "world" is used; because your world is your entire perspective, and so it is your entire understanding of realty. Without contemplation, your world is your reality. Weather you are open to the fact that so much exists outside of you or you are closed to it is a state of mind. Worlds don't change; they are like a cycle or a rut (as we sometimes call it) of doing the same things again and again, with little to no deviations. But this is happening, not on one level, but on every level. This means that it is not just when our actions are repeated, but also when our thoughts and opinions wont change.

When Adam discovered the Infinite, he found with it a whole new world. And this new world, Adam said, was "above" our world. Adam separated the two by calling his new world the "Spiritual World." And the world he was born into and lived within, "our world." He discovered this spiritual world by finding his cause of all causes in the Infinite. Here is where he understood that even his ideas, his thoughts, and every simple concept that popped into his mind existed, not as a thing, like an apple or a pear, but as information. In a more modern lens, think computers. He presumed, from his search for his cause of all causes, that everything that existed had a purpose and a place. That nothing was random; nothing was a coincidence, not a hair stray and not a pebble out of place. Everything was where it was and how it was for a tangible reason.

Just because he didn't know what the reason might be didn't

mean that it wasn't there. This he called faith, believing that there was a reason for even things that he did not understand. In other words, there was a cause. Now this did not just include every corporeal thing but even to the domain of his mind. Even every thought about the sun, moon, mountains, trees, or a really big rock. Even every thought about cause and effect. Even the thoughts about the thoughts thought about thinking itself. Each one existed purposefully in its place, not randomly. His cause of all causes was of everything and every thought of everything as well.

Here, we will return to an old example. "My city," my bubble of of perception that contains my knowledge (even opinion) of the city in which I live. It is a world (as is work or home or anything), and as a world, it is purely perception. And yes, this has been repeated multiple times (and maybe some more) because of how important the idea of a "world" is. Everything that has to do with you as a conscious being is a world. Your ideas, worlds within worlds. Your experiences, worlds within worlds. Your belongings, worlds within worlds. And this will not change. Because everything outside (different) from worlds is part of the Infinite. And since the Infinite is going to do what the Infinite is going to do concerning you, it is the "juggling of the worlds" that is your "response."

"My city" is uniquely my experiences and awareness. It is unique to me. It is different than any other "my city" that exists for anyone else, even thought the dimensions of the city did not change for any one of us.

From the lens of perspective, the worlds make up an infinite fractal of reality. Each world is a single picture, completely interconnected. every part of a world leaves an imprint on every other part. This means that if anything were to be added to a world, it would change every part of it (like the an top hat) creating a new world altogether.

We have here three names, ideas that we are using: worlds, objects, and bowls. It has been stated that these three things are all the same. The reason for the added confusion here is that while there is one "object" (as with the Infinite), the different terms refer to the "force" at work within the object. The name "object" only refers to its existence and the fact that it exists. It is not doing, being, or acting. The name "bowl" refers to its reception; it is the object that is a container of the Infinite. A bowl is "from the perspective of the Infinite." The name "world" is the object from our perspective. Or the bowl, in the hands of the child who wishes to hold the ocean. So, you see, this is not trying to be complicated for the sake of complication. It is simply a matter of the Infinite and the observer. Or God and us.

So this complicated chapter titrates to a concept introduced earlier of the bowls in order to expand on it. The bowls are used by the child to contain the ocean. The bowls are the same thing as the worlds. This is important because, before we begin to discuss what the water that fills the bowls is, we need to fully understand what this object is in its multiple facets, making sure that we are "holding" the same objects in hand. This will help us understand the "water" that fills them. This is why it is necessary to retrace this concept of worlds again (and again). There is no attainment in the Infinite without a world/bowl/vessel to contain it in.

8

Heaven and the Higher Worlds

Our introduction to physical objects is from our sensational evolution. Where we feel with our fingers, hear with our ears, and see with our eyes. We expand these senses with the numerous objects that surround us at all times. As as we grow with these new objects, new senses evolve in order to sense them, like when we have two or three apples to touch and taste and fiddle with. Our physical senses play with the apples, but our new "spiritual" senses play with the "two" (or three). The Spiritual Dimension is utterly separate from the Physical Dimension. So much so that where the Corporeal Dimension is called "Earth," the spiritual one is called "Heaven." To begin, the Spiritual Dimension is not foreign to you, even if you have heard that it is blocked by a wall or some veil. These are metaphors. The spiritual is blocked by miscommunication and misunderstanding. If you cannot see the spiritual world, there are three explanations for why. One, the spiritual world is unlike the physical world in the same way that the virtual world is different than the coding language used to write it.

Two, seeing is understanding, but only spiritually. Example: a mathematician shows you a chalkboard filled with his latest equation and asks if you can "see" it.

You look at it for a few minutes, five or six. And in a eureka moment, you see it. We use this kind of language all the time, but it is almost subconscious to what it means. Neither you nor the mathematician are confused with what it means to see. He asks if you understand his thought, and after a few minutes of contemplation, you confirm. This is the spiritual world that you cannot see. The third reason that you cannot see the spiritual world is that it is, in fact, the corporeal world that you are missing. Another example: say there is a microwave in front of you on a table. It is a microwave; nothing spiritual about it at all. But can you see it? Are you actually seeing it? And you can answer yes or no. No. Your eyes do not reach out; they accept light into them. And, whereas the microwave emits energy, it is not in the visible spectrum. Your eyes do not see the microwave; they see the light reflected off of it. It is the same with your ears and nose. Your senses receive; they do not reach out.

In addition, it is not light that your eyes send to your brain. It is a signal that needs translating. The image created in your mind is information that has gone through many different translations into many different "languages." You can see the microwave. It is right there on the table. This microwave that you are definitely seeing, however, is a spiritual object. This is the object created in your mind; it exists only in your mind, and none of the corporeal objects ("real" microwaves) are within it. But this is everything. Everything you see, touch, hear, or smell is only the objects created in and by your mind from information given to it. We just don't think about it this way.

This is why you can actually see the spiritual world. Because that microwave that you have been seeing and sensing was the spiritual microwave, not the corporeal one. You just need to understand what it is you are actually sensing.

Imagine you extend both of your hands, and in one, you hold an apple. In the other hand, you visualize an apple (pretending that you can visualize exceptionally well). One of these apples is corporeal, and the other is spiritual. We will be returning to these apples several times, but they are introduced here to say that one is made up of atoms, and electrons, and protons, while the other is made up of thought. That is the difference between the two dimensions.

And this is the reason that you can remember your microwave and past microwaves. Because (just like the penguin) it is a spiritual object that you are remembering. A spiritual object is beyond time and space and will never change, even if you drop the "real" microwave. What is the difference between a microwave and a broken microwave? In a corporeal sense, there is none. There are the same materials in the same ratios in both. And the idea that they are not in the same places as before doesn't matter because matter is always in motion. Now, this is not a technical manual for fixing microwaves, but the point being raised is that the spiritual object of the microwave is now joined (like the penguin in a top hat) by a spiritual object of the broken microwave. And because it is not a technical manual, it will be left at that.

However, regarding the technical manual, there is yet another aspect of this spiritual microwave that needs to be uncovered. That is because the microwave that you have your relationship with is not the corporeal unit, as your senses do not actually access the corporeal unit. The spiritual unit is as it exists in your mind. This means that if you were to read the technical manual, the microwave in your mind would be closer to how the microwave truly exists. This topic was mentioned earlier as the "names" of the sun. Here, we can see the "names" (or levels of understanding) of this microwave. There are levels of understanding that lead us deeper and deeper into the identity of the microwave. Here, we can ask, "What is the difference between a microwave, and 'my city?'" Your microwave is a world unto itself because it is your perception of it. Just as a name is perception from the outside, the world is from the inside.

You can think of these differences as simply as different colors. Infinite shades, within and overlapping more, infinite shades. Two colors mix to create a third, and with a third, create yet another. The city is a color, and as a shade within a shade of another color lies some electronic appliances. Every spiritual object (thought) is as a color, or shade. Or (perhaps more accurately) a frequency.

There is only one reality, and in reality, this physical dimension is merely the outer peel or papery skin of an onion. It is not a separate dimension (as dimensions are parameters of measurement) but the lowest part of the only reality. It is considered separate because of our senses, which are filled with this paper, and we cannot see the "juicy oniony layers within."

As our spiritual senses evolve, our "senses" of thought and reason, we "enter" the "heavens." The heavens are the dimensions above this physical. And the reason for the "higher and lower" is a bit of psychological alchemy. We will think of thoughts as states of matter, solid and liquid, gas and plasma. We can see solid thoughts as facts and concepts. We can understand this as solid words we used when talking about things we know and have not merely heard. Liquid thoughts can be seen as usual thoughts, feelings, and opinions, the ones that flow with the tide. Philosophy is in the air and thoughts about thoughts and purely thinkable things. As for fire, fire is passion, thoughts that are above the definition of thinking.

Remember the two apples held in each hand. Think of thought as the spiritual equivalent of atoms being physical. Thought is like the information from a computer; thought is or is not, like the 1s and 0s of binary. And just as the state of matter is determined by temperature. The state of mind is determined by frequency. This is why the higher the "temperature," the "higher" the thoughts. Higher thoughts are in higher dimensions, which are the higher levels of reality itself. As for spiritual objects, their understanding and attainment are referred to as worlds. Higher worlds, or names, reach to the root of the spiritual object, the cause of them. And as steps, cause upon causes, closer to the infinite cause of all causes from the beginning.

These levels, temperatures, or frequencies are part of reality, and it is our consciousness that separates them from reality by the distinctions of dimensions, worlds, names, and bowls. All of them being the same thing, the same object. All these different names are how they interact with the purpose and focus of the study, which is the Infinite. The dimensions measure the Infinite. The worlds experience the Infinite. The names define the Infinite. And the bowls contain the Infinite. But the Infinite, being endless, always has more to reveal. By frequency, it goes ever higher and higher. But by understanding, it goes ever deeper and deeper. And at the highest of the degrees, there are splendors even higher. And within the depths of the unknown, there are unknown depths even further. The vast depths of black space beyond the night sky are the perfect metaphor for our place in the spiritual universe. How much there is to know that we don't know. It is infinite, and as we discussed earlier, there is only one Infinite. And there is only one reality. There is only one reality, and our bowls are eagerly digging away at it. What fills the bowls (our understanding) is called the "known" (as opposed to the unknown) because it is unknown how information goes from outside of our "bowls" to the inside of them. It is the "will" of the Infinite that it does so. And so, it could be said that knowledge is the offspring of the unknown.

Neither the Infinite, the ocean, nor the water changes when it goes from unknown to known. Only we change. Realty doesn't alter; the only thing different is the perceiver. This is the meaning of the worlds, bowls, names, and the objects themselves. We cannot break down the Infinite to fit into our understandings, so we instead build ourselves up to attain greater and greater heavens. We create these spiritual objects for the work of elevating ourselves. The bowls we hold are not up to the task of containing the ocean, but when we smack them on the surface of the water, we can know of the ocean by the waves that we make. And this is the study of God. Smacking waters and making waves. Metaphorically, of course, and physically, when no one is watching.

The only part that is moving in this static spiritual reality is us. Our consciousness or mind, our understandings or desires. Our wisdom, and eventually, our souls. It is how we transfer from one world to the next that we are studying, how we grow closer and closer to the Infinite that created us in the beginning. And just as the unknown is responsible for "giving" us knowledge, it is the higher world that creates the growth within this, our lower world. It is us that move from one world to another, and it is the heavens, that were always there (even though we couldn't not see them) that instigate the transfer. From the outside, all that transpired is that we stepped over the threshold from one world to another. But for us, it was a mighty leap.

9

Destroying Worlds

Understanding the idea of the spiritual world and the study of God is something. Knowing that God is Infinite and Unknown is fine and good. Knowing that another word for "perception" is "world" is helpful in certain circles. And knowing that our understanding of things could be referred to as bowl can be awesome at times. But for those who are looking for something real, of answers of some kind, it can be easy to grow indignant with all of the jargon and platitudes. The technical details mean nothing without the feels. It is not enough to know what, but to know how. To begin with, this aim (there will be deeper delving in later chapters) is the orientation of this chapter. Because, though what is really happening from the perspective of reality is the conscious mind merely seeping from one world to another (higher) world, from inside, from our perspective, it is the destroying of worlds.

It is this way from two angles. From our world, we experience a flood of information. That changes everything that we saw, even to the way that we saw it. Our world is completely interdependent, and every aspect is bound to every other aspect by way of familiarity. If anything is added to our world, it is assimilated by and with every aspect. Nothing is "out of place." If it cannot be assimilated, it is ignored or is as a poison that slowly rots our world from the inside. For these reasons, our worlds will never become the higher worlds. They are completely separated. It is our perception, and something that is also only our perception is our pride. Arrogance, fear, and anxiety are also symptoms of perspective, forces that make up the walls of our world. Our world never merges with the higher. And from the second angle, the higher world is not new. It was and always was. After all, the Infinite was the first, and by cause and effect of the dimensions of reality down to the world above and our world below. The world above came first, and our world is its effect, almost like a submarine trapped under the water's surface. If it is punctured, the water flows in quite violently. It is also like the nest, tree, forest, and mother bird outside of the baby bird's egg. A loving world just waiting to be explored. And the instant the baby bird breaks his head out of his egg, his eyes are flooded with light, his ears with sound, his nostrils with scents, and his entire little body with air. But either way, positive or not, it is a flood of information, that destroys everything one thought about reality and one's own past world.

Our world to a higher world. Earth to heaven. Physical to spiritual. The ideas and concepts have been set. Now, we attempt to make them real within our minds (worlds).

We have contemplated "my city." This will be our stand-in "our world," our personal world, lower world, Earth, or physical world. And the name of the Higher world is "our city."

Our city is not the highest world; it is not the city as it exists in reality. Because we (none of us) have no understanding of it down to the subatomic aspects, which are a necessary part of reality. Instead, our city is the world from the perspective of the inhabitants. The people who live within it. This may sound weird because a perspective is usually that of a single observer. But your perspective is given by two eyes, and ours is given by multiple people. It is actually the same thing. The only difference is that none of us are aware of the perception of anyone other than ourselves. This doesn't matter because the events that occur within our city happen because of the direct actions of other people. Just because we don't attempt to see the world through their eyes, does not change the fact that they have an effect on us. And such an effect that our world would be completely different without them. Just because we don't attempt to see the world through their eyes doesn't mean that they don't have sights and feels of their own and exist independently from us. And yet, we don't give them credit because we are unaware of their perspective. My city, though unique, would not exist without the "our city" that is above it. And it is as insignificant as a single chicken egg in a coup.

The world of my city is filled with all of its lesser worlds within it, even down to my microwave oven. It is an egg birthed into an entire world. And here we find ourselves stuck because it is our perception, the sight of our eyes, the sound of our ears, and the touch of our skin. Whatever we try to cram into our worlds with us, until we learn to see with new eyes and hear with new ears and touch with new skin, will only assimilate. Without new senses, spiritual senses, we will never be able to see the whole world beyond the threshold of our own. This knowledge may cause a kind of revolution within us. A thrashing about from us, within our worlds. There may be a struggle of sorts. We may seek to burn our world with fire. Burn it to ashes with the fire of passion. Or perhaps wash it away with water. Drown it with study and with books. Or even to blow it away with harsh winds. However, try as we might, none of these methods will work because they will all add to our perception. Every sight will go into our eyes, and every sound into our ears. The same that is part of the perception of this world. It is a part of this world, and this world will never rise. The world won't rise, but we can. There does seem to be a discrepancy here, however, because a world is perception, and how can we leave our perception behind?

Now, this struggle is not without purpose. It is like the struggle of a chick. And it is how the egg breaks. But it is important to keep in mind that it is not the struggle that is important; it is the breaking of the shell. But it is also similar to the mere growing of the chicken. When it reaches a certain size, the breaking (even the struggle) is a natural occurrence. So is our mini-revolution, our desire to find some thing, some answer. Our search, while feeling like a struggle, it is also natural growth. It doesn't feel like natural growth, but in times of clarity, it helps to understand the laws that overlooking the growth of every tree and life of every creeping thing that creeps on the face of the Earth. These laws are universal and perfect, and you are not outside of them. Everything is in its place, even growth, whether it is pleasant or painful. As we grow, and struggle, and search for something that we don't even know, our perspectives change. We dissociate from our physical eyes to our spiritual eyes. We transition from our world to another. In reality, we are stepping over the threshold from one world to another. But it feels like the destruction of our world. This leaving of the old world and the old perspective.

This "destruction" of the past ways. This is the process that we call growth.

10

Attaining Higher Worlds

The study of God is about devoting time and attention to acquiring knowledge of the Infinite. And there is no attainment (acquisition) of knowledge without a bowl (desire) to receive it. Bowls are an integral part of the study of God, as there is no study whatsoever without them. The first step in the study is the creation of a bowl. And in the same way that clay bowls are made by our hands, spiritual bowls are made by spiritual hands (concentration, study, "hands-on approach" kind of thing). The study of God is simply the focused intention to the endless point; it is about the water outside of the bowl and not the water within it. As was stated before, what is happening on the surface of the mind is less important than what is happening beneath. Because what is happening is the growth of the consciousness. The perceiver becoming self-aware of their perception. Here, we are going to create (or introduce) a new Spiritual Object. A name for the self-aware perceiver, as the word "perceiver" does not differentiate if it is presently self-aware or not. And being self-aware is the key state of being for growth and the study. The perceiver is like the pupil of the eye. Perception is what passes through it, even if, with the use of a mirror, it passes through itself. Of this occurrence, it will never know. The perceiver is not aware if it is looking at itself unless it is self-aware. A name must be made for a self-aware perception as opposed to mere perception perceived. And that name (created here and not important in itself) will be "Pilgrim." This name will be used much more in later chapters, but it is necessary that it is created here in the chapters on worlds and bowls and names and things. For the rest of the book, the Pilgrim is the point that we can fasten to ourselves for a more personal understanding. Pilgrim is the state of being aware of your current state or being self-aware. And for further clarification, for example, the study of God is Pilgrim.

What is the meaning of worlds being destroyed if worlds are spiritual objects and spiritual objects are eternal? Worlds, names, and bowls, are all descriptors of the same object and are, in fact, spiritual objects (thoughts) themselves. This is because the worlds are an illusion in the same way we just created a name out of the blue, with no prior causality. Something that just happened and had no reason to happen, a random occurrence. This perception is purely illusory. The cause of the name was a need for clarification. And there was a need for clarification because of an idea. There was an idea because of the opening of a book. There was an opening of a book because of the curiosity to a closed book. There was a closed book because of a search for an answer. There was a search for an answer because of a desire for knowledge. There was a desire for knowledge because of an observation of the surroundings. There was an observation because of self-awareness. There was a self-awareness because of an identity of self. There was an identity of self because of a society of selves. And there was a society of selves because of a common goal of survival. And there was a common goal of survival because of being alive in the first place. And there was life in the first place because of the evolution of the planet. And there was the evolution of a planet because of the gravity of a forming sun. And there was the gravity of a forming sun because of the will of the Infinite. There is no randomness; there is just a lack of understanding due to the limited size of our bowls. Bigger bowls lead to a greater awe of the Infinite. Bigger bowls lead to a closer relationship with the Infinite. Bigger bowls lead us closer to God.

Cause and effect, that is the gist; there was a cause. That is reality. And our perception was wrong. The perception is an illusion. The object is real; the object exists as and is described by its layers and layers of names. We did not create this name out of the blue, but its cause is above our perception. Another way of saying this is that God is not surprised. When a world is destroyed, we can look back (think back) at it and remember. Because the object remains, but the perspective does not. We do not see it as we did before because we are not the same perceiver as we were before. This can be hard to grasp because before we became self-aware to this degree, we were our own worlds. From our (past) perspective, I am my world, and my world is me. I am my perception, and my perception is me. And I can never part with what is the same me as me; I cannot divide myself down the middle. The idea is lunacy. Only when we become the observer of our own perception do we see our world for what it is. Merely a shell made of clay. And this is what is meant by, "the study of God is Pilgrim."

The worlds are illusions because the reality is the objects

themselves. But we can never see the objects themselves; only the information is transcribed to us by our senses. So, we study these "worlds" in order to know the objects within them, we need the illusions because they tell us all that we hear about the objects, the reality itself. But the illusions aren't real, leaving us as drowning in deep waters. It is our spiritual senses that can see the objects themselves. These are our reason, knowledge, faith and understanding, hope and love. These senses, which emerge from our open-minded self-awareness, can see like new eyes and hear like new ears. These senses help us to know a deeper world, a layer closer to the reality of the Infinite. To become a Pilgrim on the road to heaven. This is the study of God.

This is because to be self-aware is to be in a state of growth. And the mere growth of the mind is the reality of the study of God. Now, one may say that one could be self aware without being aware of growth. But the answer to that is in the level of self-awareness. For at one time, a person was not even aware of their own body. They were not aware of themselves at all Just a baby sitting in their crib, looking outward. Their hands were mere emanations of the unknown universe that brought their desires of mastication to their open mouths. But then they grew and became aware of their hands, even to the point of individual finger movement. Their hands still bring items of curiosity towards them, but now it was by their control, their own will. And slowly, their sense of self grew closer and closer of their feet and legs. With the understanding that their desire was not naturally growing closer to them by an unknown will but that they were moving of their own will. They became aware of their body. And in time of their head. In time, they could recognize themselves in a mirror, not just their point of identity, but that the eyes were tools of their own. As they grew, they began to identify themselves as their body until they became aware of their thoughts. They were not a body observing a place; they were a mind observing a body. And upon that awareness, the mind began to control the body. Now, the body does not act purely on its desires and instincts; instead, the mind uses it for even greater purposes. This growth is the only growth. And it continues, and repeats, layer over layer. Becoming self-aware means your spiritual observing of your physical. Your soul observing your spiritual. All levels upon levels of self-awareness. Worlds of past perceptions dying, breaking. Falling away and turning into clay while the soul ascends to the heavens. Growing a new, spiritual body, walking on its surface as a new Earth, its new world. A new heaven above, to begin the process all over again. As one step closer to the Infinite Endless, cause of all causes.

III

Love

11

God Is Love

What is the infinite that it can know love? And why do we say God is love and not loving? There is so much separation between the character of God that we have seen and heard from the mouths and lives of others. There is such a difference between this Avatar, and the Infinite that Adam spoke of. And it feels as if they are as separate as east from west. And yet we are expected to believe that this is all within the plan of the Infinite, of God himself because it is part of his will. Everything that we have witnessed, done by, or in the name of, this character is part of his ineffable will. While all that can be known of this Infinite Endless being is well defined in the words "infinite" and "endless," we want to go deeper, in understanding of this being, even while he seems to be "pushing" us away. And all the while, our definition of love (which must also fall into the confines of his "will") does not hold to his actions. So who is this Infinite that he can know love? And what was it that Adam called "love" in the first place?

Whilst looking for the beginning cause of all causes, Adam

discovered the Infinite. The words "discovered" and "invented" can be interchanged here, as in "Adam invented God." The reason for this is that our entire understanding of the idea of Infinity is quite finite. Even the sentence "goes on forever," ends. So, we can see here that our idea of infinity and Infinity itself are two separate things. Real infinity is discovered, but the spiritual object called "infinity" is created. For example, we can use math. The Sumerians invented/discovered math around 3000 BC. The Sumerians invented math because there was nothing called "math" before the Sumerians invented it. The Sumerians discovered math because mathematics is the universal language of reality and, therefore, cannot be invented because it itself wrote the universe. This is what we mean by these two words are interchangeable. If you believe that math was invented, then Adam invented God. But if you believe that math was discovered, then Adam, whilst looking for the beginning cause of all causes, discovered the Infinite.

But what was the Infinite? And how did he find it if he started from the finite? As we know, if we begin counting from a finite number, even by multiples or exponents, we will never reach Infinity, even if we count for Infinity. Adam found the Infinite because he looked for him using a reverse method. In a way, he used the scientific method. He theorized, and in that theory, there was a void where an object had to be. The theory was that "cause and effect" was itself an effect that needed to be caused by an initial cause. Now, this initial cause does not have a cause itself because it would not be outside the effect called "cause and effect." This initial cause is the object in the void of his theory and is the cause of all causes. And this initial cause, being the cause of all causes, is all that Adam knew about the Infinite that he discovered. It had no cause itself, and so it always was. It itself does not cause effects within itself, so it cannot change or have ever changed in all the "time" that it was. And so this infinite and endless thing that existed in the void of his theory, he called apropos, Infinite Endless.

Infinity and endlessness were all that Adam knew about this object that he had discovered. And he contemplated it endlessly. But knowing nothing about what it was, he could only build upon what it was not. For example, it isn't a book because a book has pages that can be in different positions. An open book is the effect of a change in a closed book. Not the best example, but Adam had a lot of time on his hands and thought a lot about what this object was not, and he surely thought at some point of why it wasn't a book (or scroll, probably). And this is why he referred to it simply as "endless," because every other name he could think of had an aspect to it, unaligned to a changeless Infinity. By way of cutting away all that it was not, he defined what it was. The Infinite Endless is one object. Now, the word "object" feels small and impersonal, so the word "entity" also works. However, the word entity might add a frame of personality and identity, both concepts that have aspects of change and finitude. The words "infinite," and "endless" represent all the personality and identity that this entity possesses, which is why we are using the small and impersonal word "object" here. The Endless is a single object, not any form of a combination of other objects. And it is an unchanging object, having no system of cause and effect within or around itself. And it is endless, meaning that it is causeless. Now, there must be a little vernacular juggling here. It is not that the Infinite is an object that is causeless. It is that the object that is causeless is the Infinite. In other words, the penguin in a top hat is different than the penguin. This is an important point to make because the endless cause of all causes is a spiritual object. And as we learned with the penguin, a different thought of the penguin, no matter how slight, is a whole new penguin. The Endless is endless and nothing besides.

So this endless, unchanging, un-altering, and eternal thing is the Infinite. And because it was the beginning cause of all causes, it was alone until it wasn't. Another depth of discovery that Adam delved into with the same technique was not what it was but what it was not. His Endless Infinite was a spiritual object. Adam found that this object had to be capable of creating (causing) everything that was created. In other words, being the cause of everything that was caused. And being so without any change in or of itself. This means that this spiritual object was, by its nature and purpose, creation. Adam proposed that his Infinite was a single thought of creation. But not just a continual belching out of creative essence because that would have caused nothing but a universe filled with this blank and static essence. And if that were the case, then there would have to be some other thing that caused that static essence to become starts and planets and people and toes and all things that exist. And that other thing would be (by definition) another thing that existed besides the Infinite thing, making two things, which would make the Infinite, not the infinite. And whatever caused the two things to exist would be the infinite thing that Adam discovered. And yes, that was a complicated sentence, but it was a necessary one to illustrate how Adam discovers the Infinite in reverse. There is no way to know how many instances of cause and effect exist between our existence as an effect and the initial cause of all causes itself. And it is possible that many of them appear to be the initial cause itself.

This "thought of creation" had to be something more. Adam believed this because everything in existence is caused by an effect, and nothing that exists is random or out of place. Everything is as it is meant to be. An example of this is if you were to stand on the top of a staircase with a very large bucket full of marbles and pour the marbles down the staircase. Knowing the final position of every marble would be an impossibility for you, but physics would be unfazed. At no point during the cascade of the marbles would reality break or even lag. Physics would calculate the fall, bounce, and roll of every single marble concurrently and without fail. And no marble would find itself out of its place, outside the causality of the universe. Because this is the universe, many objects, reacting to other objects. But this example is not just with the marbles. Because even the desire and curiosity within you to collect the marbles and place them in the very large bucket in the first place is part of the very same causality of the universe. The idea did not magically appear in your mind; it was not "out of place," and the physics of the Spiritual Dimension was not fazed. Even if you were to stand on top of the staircase and feign the toss, the cause of the feign, or the toss itself, is of causality. And on a side note, this is what is meant in the words "God is not mocked." All was caused by the initial cause of all causes, the Infinite.

This "thought of creation" was not as simple as "create." It had to be more complex because it had to create what was created. It had to begin the cascade of cause and effect that was created and exists today all around us. In a way, that is the core of what he is; God is creator, or creation itself. Adam believed that the Infinite had to be the thing that caused all other things to cascade from itself without changing itself. The

Infinite is spiritual, a thought. In other words, it is mind, and the universe is mental. And the Infinite is the single thought behind, around, and beginning it all. Or, the single thought that is behind, around, and beginning it all is the Infinite. Adam thought quite a lot about this thought and came up with an idea of what this thought could be. Adam proposed it to be a thought that created a receiver for its own thinking. Or a thought that thought about a thing to think about. Now, these words don't mean much and do nothing to explain what this thought is, and Adam realized this. So he put in terms of emotion that this thought is the desire to do good to its creation. This spiritual object, called Infinite, creates a receiver for it to fill. And this object created by this thought is created of this thought. And so, it will desire to create an object to fill. This spiritual object creates creation . It is, in this way, self-replicating, self-perpetuating, and cascading. This is what Adam called Love, the infinite, endless desire to fill its created being, that creates, within its very nature, a creature to fill.

'We can define love as the force that holds things together, from gravity, to romance, to quantum entanglement. It is pull; it is the will to be together. And it is desire itself. It is that which is God, and it is the only thought that grows, and multiplies. It is growth, the force that drives growth, and the only spiritual object that is self-perpetuating. It is what creates us and draws us towards our creator. And this is what is meant by God is love.

12

Leaf, Sun, Primordial Singularity

What is Love and can it be infinite? And how can we find a tangible piece that we can grasp and understand? We don't want to continue with an ethereal conversation about hypothesis and conjecture. At some point, this needs to merge with the lives we live and not speculations in our dreams and delusions.

There is no way to know how many instances of cause and effect exist between our existence as an effect and the initial cause of all causes itself. And it is possible that many of them appear to be the initial cause itself. In the same way, a logarithmic spiral seems to "repeat" itself. If something appears to give life to all that exists and be the center of all that exists, we will find ourselves tempted to call it God. Case in point: sun worship. We must be careful here because these ideas lead to death, and that will be explained in a later chapter. Earlier, when introducing Adam and the Infinite, which he discovered, we said that these days, it is referred to as the Big Bang. Is this accurate? Yes, no, and maybe. Let's expound on this.

Let us begin by contemplating the presence of the Big Bang. It is the cause of all causes of this dimension. It is the beginning of everything we know about this universe. And we want to keep in mind that the Big Bang is not visible to us at all. Even the latest scientific module is not a picture of it, but a description of its cascade by the parameters of billions of years. It explains how matter is formed, followed by the stars and then the planets. It explains how our universe emerged from its source. It is at the center of this dimension, in the same way that the Infinite is at the center of reality. We will keep this in the mind's eye. Keep it present in our focus as we "fall" lower and smaller. Visualizing in our minds the expanse of the universe while keeping focus on the Bang that birthed it all. Contemplate the galactic clusters, each one containing billions of galaxies filled with stars. See our "Milky Way" and count the stars within. How massive is their number. And while keeping within our mind our focus on the cascade that caused all to exist. See our sun, but as a dot within the arm of our galaxy. See it in its grandeur, consider the size of the sun, and hold in mind its measure. Then, think of the Earth as it exists, seeing in mind its true magnificent size and how many trillions of lives it supports. Try to hold numbers that help you think of the true size of any one of these objects. See yourself witnessing the universe, standing in a grassy field beside a tall tree. And while remembering the Singularity above, see, falling from the branch of the tree, a single leaf.

We will hold this leaf in hand, and, as with the sun before and the universe above, we will "ask" of it, its name. Not the label of which we refer to it, being "leaf." But of its reality, its name in deepest truth and highest splendor. As we look deeper into the leaf, we can see past its color, midrib, and veins. We can see past its epidermis and into its cellular structure. But even this level is not its truth, as we can go deeper into each and every cell, past the wall and membrane, and into its own self and body. Deep within its nucleus, we breach into an entirely new universe that our eyes can no longer strain to witness and far beyond even that. Layers upon layers of magnitude down into the many worlds below the subatomic. Deeper below these worlds is where its true name is written.

From here, we look up and back up all the way. We fly back to the highest heights of the universe. We return to the Primordial Singularity (a fancier name for the Big Bang). Remember that in the Spiritual Dimension there is no time or place (eternal penguin), so the Big Bang is not a when but a where (and the where being as a frequency). And the where is as it pertains to Adam's Infinite Endless. So, what does this actually mean? Is the beginning stage of our universe the same as the infinite cause of all causes? This is an unknown, but in times before, the sun was used as an example. Infinite light, or always shining. Cause of all causes, or cause of all growth and life in the (at the time) known universe. We will use the Primordial Singularity in the same way.

But first, before we begin, we need to prepare ourselves and protect ourselves from a great danger. In the corporeality of this dimension, making a false comparison is a rather small faux-pas (we talked about this earlier, about pointing and speaking and of names). It is like comparing apples and oranges. But in the spiritual, it is deadly. Because a spiritual object can be created but never destroyed. And if we remember the penguin in a bowler cap, this concept will be fully understood. From our studies of the microwave, there was the real microwave, and then there was the spiritual microwave. And the spiritual microwave existed only in our world (perception). We create

ual objects within our world and not outside of it. This means that if we take an object and say that it is God, we are no longer looking toward God, but toward the object that we created and that exists within our world. Following it will only lead deeper into our world and not toward heaven. It is like jumping into a river in order to grasp and hold the moon, because of the reflection you perceive on the surface of the water. A reflection is both beautiful and wonderful and is not harmful in any way. On the contrary, it is quite useful in many ways. But it is of little value to the calculations of rocketry. If one confuses the reflection on the surface of the water with the moon in the sky, the force of one's dreams may cause them to drown.

God is love. The Infinite is the cascade of the thought of creation. And the thought of creation creates creation. This can be seen as the sun that is light and creates light. Or in the Singularity that is matter and creates matter. Some teachers, while contemplating the words of Adam, used the sun in this way as an example of Adam's Endless Infinite. Even calling the infinite thought of creation, "light," causes a lot of confusion. This reflection in the waters caused many to loose their way and even drown. But Adam called it Love, which also caused a lot of (although different) confusion. Essence, Ether, Spirit, and even Mana have all been used, each name causing different amounts of different confusion. If we were to call this thought, "Petrol," it would cause no end to the false analogies and lead to errant ideas and presumptions, even leading some out to vast deserts to perish. So, we are going to try not to introduce a new metaphor that cannot hope to point to the true idea of the thought of creation. But what if we assume that the emanation of the Primordial Singularity was not material but instead spiritual, the building blocks of matter itself, energy, but of a higher frequency? Or, in unscientific terms, the "infinite thought of creation." In this way, we will "visualize" the creator, thought of creation cascading into the known universe and down to the lives we live and the worlds that surround us.

Does this make God tangible? No, because there is no way to know how many iterations of causality exist between the initial cause of all causes and our existence as an effect. Even though this is not God, this is as God, and this is his name in the same way that the logarithmic spiral grows, and seemingly replaces itself as the perspective of the viewer grows larger. In this same way, the universe is expanding before our growing intellect (understanding, or spiritual eyes). His true names are "Unknown," and "Unknowable." And even "unnameable" can be tossed in the pile. This is so because there is no attainment without a vessel to contain it in. And there are no vessels (bowls) that can contain him.

God, in reality, can only draw so close to our tangible existence because the Infinite cannot fit into our minds, just like the ocean cannot fit into any of our variously sized bowls. It is, however, not pointless to try, if only to remind ourselves of the universe that remains an eternal constant around us. When was the last time you truly contemplated the galactic cluster in which you find yourself? It is, after all, your deep truth and high splendor. It must not be forgotten because this knowledge is your true self. Everything else is a mere reflection on the surface of the waters. And if you are not careful, you may drown, seeking your purpose and place in a swim and not in flight.

The Primordial Singularity is not God; neither is the sun, nor the leaf. But this is because we have no ability to utter his true name. The name of his deepest truths and highest splendors. But if we could, if we had the ability to say it, to know it, and to read it, we would speak it of the leaf, as its true name, and of the sun, and of the Big Bang as well. Because it would be the true name of Infinity and the true scope of eternity. It would be the beginning, and it would be the end. But because our tongues don't stretch that far. Adam called it Love, and others call it Light. Essence, Ether, Spirit, or Mana. And maybe even Petrol.

13

Gravity, Romance, and Quantum Entanglement

Over the last few chapters, we seem to have strayed from our beginning topic. As when we began, God was "as a friend, companion, or even sojourner" and the like. We began with a more personal conversation and then fell to the static and unmovable. Of God as unknowable and unseen. This is the way we are introduced to God in the first place, as in the lethargic sermons or drab t-shirts. The way God can be as a brick that you lay on your desk or hang on your wall. As to remind yourself that you do, or at least did, believe in something sometime. The God in the boring sermons from our childhoods. But this is before we hear from his "personal" witnesses and those who have "met" him in their lives. Before we gain our own yearning for such an encounter, most of us can say with pure honesty that we would love to meet some strange, all-knowing being who can answer our questions about existence and lay our worries to rest. Or to tell us even simpler things, like what we are supposed to be doing with our lives and who we are supposed to be. Just an assurance that we are on some "right track" in our daily lives. And while this is not the God that we have been introduced to, it is the only God that we desire to meet. And we could even say, a bit more heretically, that it is the only God worthy of devotion. Even to the extent that with or without ever knowing him, we are devoted to the idea of a tangle purpose. And this is what we mean by "yearning."

We have talked about God and tried to paint a kind of picture of his magnificence. But keep in mind that even the wonders of the Primordial Singularity only exist to us as transcribed by our perception, and reality is always above and out of reach. And it is this constant reaching that is our growth and evolution. So important is this reaching that the sages of old named it "righteousness" and its lack, "wicked." It is this reaching that is within us, as is the entire cascade itself outside. As the thought of creation is timeless and all-encompassing, so should be our reaching for higher knowledge, understanding, and attainment. It is for this purpose that God meets us inside our own worlds; he creates an Avatar of his own self to bring us out. To break us out of our own perception into a greater world and a greater dimension of reality.

As children, we are bored with this static, lethargic character but remember it as the first God we know. But what if this God is no God whatsoever? What if God is not just personal but only personal? Perhaps it is as they say, "God has no grandchildren." God cannot be passed from one to another. If we take these church chores from our childhood and remove them from our definition of God, and by this, we mean removing other gods from our contemplation of God. Or we remove what is not God, even if it is what we were told is God to and by someone else. If we remove this from our search for God, we may find ourselves searching for something that we would never call God. We have to come to the realization that an Infinite God will not look like the fat man in a white robe that we may visualize. In fact, the "yearning" that we have, even that we cannot articulate, is not for a fat man in a robe at all. Our relationship with the Infinite is not inherited or discovered. It exists as assuredly as does our conscious state, only it sits unnamed. No one can name it for us. So if we put aside all that is not of the Infinite, "wipe the slate" as it were, and listen for this yearning, we will hear the Infinite surrounding us. We will "hear" what we can only call the "voice" of God. And we will meet his Avatar.

And this is that friend, the trace information or ideas. The thoughts, whatever they may be, that breaks us out of our own heads and into a grander world. This "water" uses the analogy of the viscosity of thought. And the more we anthropomorphize this water or mix it into the land to make clay, the easier it becomes to break free of the world (perceptions). It is like going to visit a friend at their house, instead of tracking out into the darkness and unknown. It can be scary to contemplate the universe in its size and grandeur, even by that of a single leaf. But that is why God comes to us, or to phrase it in a different way, we could say that "the universe can be seen to exist as" the connections. "God is love" refers not only to the Cascade of Causality but to the essence as well. Love is the force that draws together.

The "thought of creation" is not only to create but to fill. Now, while this can be hard to see in nature, this can be hard to see past with the Avatar of God. We can easily humanize God to such a point that he is unable to help us break out of our own perspective. And then we can draw him down and further

...a as a hammer to our causes, all the while knowing nothing of the higher causes and higher goals. We can be caught up in our own difficulties and use all the aid that could help us escape to entrench ourselves. This kind of language might be foreign to you concerning the creator, but that is because of our humanizing of him. Attempt to look past the human and see the anthropomorphization, and you will be able to see the state of mind that we are discussing.

Is this using the same word twice? Possibly. But these things can be difficult when discussing spiritual ideas because we use so few words so many times each. So here we will try to define our terms. To humanize God is to make him like us. But to anthropomorphize him is to overlay our understanding of ourselves onto him. If they appear to be the same thing, in a manner of speaking, they are. It is only on the intent that we are trying to focus. An example here is if you hold your hands out in front of your face, one above the other. The one above represents God, and the one below represents you. The desire is to bring the two together. Humanizing God is to take the top hand and lower it to the bottom, reducing God to be attainable to you. Anthropomorphizing God is raising the lower hand up to the top one. The proper intent is to raise ourselves to the presence of God and not lower him to our base natures. We can see God as our relationship with everything outside of our perspective (we can see God as reality). And the Avatar is a gift from God that lead us to understand ourselves in him. But how does that make God a friend?

All that exists does so within the Infinite. By the will of the Infinite, is to say it another way. A third way: Everything that exists is the Infinite, and a fourth: The Infinite is the all. And now, from the perspective of the self. There is you, and you exist within your own world (perspectives and perceptions). And all that exists for you is your perspectives and perceptions. Nothing exists within your world that is not your perspectives and perceptions, and nothing but your perspectives and perceptions exist from the perspective of your world. And so we appear to have two entities, the Infinite and the You. The infinite is endless and unchanging. And you are only what you can perceive and are entrapped in your own understanding. You are what you can perceive and only what you can perceive, and nothing outside of your conception can enter. Two separate things. Two different (unchanging) entities.

But then there is the Avatar, not the one thing, and not the other. An offspring of both, you could say. The Avatar comes to you as you are and at your level. The Avatar brings you to a higher understanding of what we are naming here: the anthropomorphic. By his desire, this Avatar is a greater friend to you than any earthly companion can be. Because any earthly companion only exists within our perception, and so is of your world, and cannot make you rise.

Now there can be some confusion here, as God was earlier introduced by the name God. By the word God, and by the identifier God. You might think that this God is the entity spelled G-O-D. But we have wrestled with this opponent before, and with a little more vernacular juggling, it is not that the Avatar comes into your world and leads you by the hand to higher understandings. It is, instead, that what comes into your world and leads you by the hand to a higher understanding is the Avatar. God is the Infinite, and all that exists is within him. There is only one Infinite, even though he goes by many names, and there is only one Avatar, even though he comes by many faces. Anything that draws you out of yourself and bids you reach for higher attainments and understandings is the Avatar sent by God to draw you unto himself. Or, that is the Avatar, an effect of the Endless Universe, as the force of gravity that draws us closer to the sun. The same force that holds everything together is the force we have come to know as love.

God is reality, the thought of creation, and wants you to grow. Growth is reaching for higher and far higher understandings and attainments. The force that draws you to reach for these understandings and attainments is the Avatar, and the attainments themselves are the anthropomorphic understanding of the Infinite itself. And the entire process is the inevitable will of the Infinite itself. Or of God himself. These words are only a matter of parlance. Love is the force of connection that brings two things together all across the universe through differing mediums as gravity, romance, and quantum entanglement. These are the definitions of the force here called "love." And this is the meaning of the words, "God is love."

14

On the Cosmic Horrors

A long time ago, there is a man sitting beneath a tree, sharpening with a stone, the blade of his spear. This man is a hunter, seasoned, but not old. And he has been hunting in these woods since boyhood. He has tracked deer, and elk, and bison. Fought bears and wolves, snakes, and panthers. He has proven himself in engagements, time and time again. He is now waiting for sight of a large bull, a worthy offering to bring to a festival of his people. He has been waiting hours, but he is a patient hunter. He has seen the tracks of this bull, and has set his intentions upon him. And he will be victorious, it is only a matter of time. And he is a patient hunter. But then, to his ears, from far deep in the woods, comes an unfamiliar sound. From the hunting grounds of his entire life, the place of his childhood where he tracked moose with his father, and grandfather. Trees through which he could find his way blind, deaf and one-legged. The woods that is his home, and his temple. These trees, his mother, and his lover. Whose every sound of nature, animal, and insect, not one unfamiliar to his ears. Not one smell or gone unsniffed or unseen. A seasoned hunter from within his own forest home hears an unfamiliar growl. He grips his spear tightly, ready to face this unseen foe, ears trained on the foreign howl. From the depth and volume, this creature must be very large. The bull is banished from his mind as now he thinks of the others who hunt and play in these woods. Of his son, just learning the ways. He stands, and steps boldly toward to wailing monster. It is loudly bellowing from deep in the forest thicket. And from the sound, its throat must be huge. Bigger than any bull and meaner than a great wolf. His spear shakes in hand, but he walks on, wits ever about him as his unseen enemy rages and thrashes about. The sounds coming from deep in the woods are terrible. He hopes others have heard it. Perhaps other hunters are nearby. The hunter does not want to face this creature alone. But he knows he must, for who knows what destruction this malefactor could bring to his village?

The demolition continues in the thick trees, and he hears two loud rumblings. And he sees in his mind a monstrous creature, bipedal. He sees it stand like a man but twice as tall, no, thrice. There is no time to return home for help from other hunters, he is here alone and alone must face the beast. As he draws closer, he can see in the far trees what appears to be a shadow. A massive animal, far larger than any bear, but he is forcibly impacted by the smell. A stench most foul. And otherworldly, earthy, and fishy, of both blood and carrion. These are not found in the smells of this forest, these are not familiar. It must be the reek of some dark power. This is no natural beast but of some foul creation. He sees it in his mind with large claws and teeth jagged. Hide thick and fur matted; his spear will do him no good. But there is no one else. If he cannot fell this

beast, then it will tare mass devastation to all that he lu
he marches on. The light of the setting sun plays tricks wi
the shadows. they are not empty, he is not alone. Does this
monstrosity have minions, an army to beckon to its call? Is it
as some lord of some nether realm? There are no sounds of
the forest here; even the birds and insects are silent. Even they
have abandoned him. Terror grips deep in his stomach as he
knows he is soon to die. He will do his duty, and if he is unable,
perhaps he can injure this demon so that some other hunter
can overcome it. That is his duty, to injure the beast, even if
just to dull its fangs with his meat. The hunter steps into the
clearing and witnesses a sick bear, "firing" from both ends. The
rancid smell is clearly rotten fish and bad mushrooms. And in
this moment, the world is dispelled. After a moment to catch
his breath and still his pounding chest, the hunter turns and
begins his walk home. Laughing to himself at the funniest sight,
and the happiest tale, to tell for generations.

What is fear that is can exist in the presence of an Infinite
God? God is the unknown, and not only is our understanding
of him within the unknown, but the unknown itself is within
God. It is a very small sphere of our knowledge, and most
of that is just opinion masquerading as knowledge. And so
we must respect the fact that this Infinite that we have been
discussing for some time is unknown and unknowable. And
this unknowable is an uncompromising force of creation. Fear
is an appropriate response. Fear is good; it protects us from
what will cause us harm or death. Fear is good; it guides us
to safety and keeps us alive. It keeps us from the pleasures of
creation in which we are not yet capable of reveling. Because
the Unknown Infinite is the cascade of an uncompromising
force of creation. And not all of it is acceptable to us as light and

beauty, in the same way that not all fruit is sweet to our tastes. Some fruit is bitter or toxic when eaten. The beauty within it is in its power and in death. So its beauty is to be respected and its taste avoided. The same God created the pleasure of the sweetness in a berry and the pleasure of the heat in a pepper and of the bitterness in the foul radishes.

This God is unknown, not vacant, but full of strange wonders and terrors. We can imagine, deep in the darkness of space, a rouge planet. Heated from its burning core. We can ponder what forms of creatures writhe on its surface and in its waters. We can fathom what form of life evolved in the darkness to hunt and to kill. What monsters lurk in the caves and the starlit shadows. What lives lived in the darknesses of the underground and in the caves within caves. What hatreds have emerged for the far illuminates? Of what form would intelligence emerge? What mad mutation of mathematics and physics will be scrawled on the slate and the stone. What mind sits scheming to reach out to the stars and extinguish their light? And are these the splendors that God has in store for his enlightened light bearers? This is the inevitable thought of creation, growth and eternal growing, far into the endless sky. It is the will of God, to face the unknown.

So, let us put ourselves in the sandals of the seasoned hunters. Sandals we hope we never have to wear. Because for the entire trek into the thicket, every step, deep down to the forest clearing, there was nothing but fear and terror. It is only at the end that any relief can come. But who knows what is at the end? If it were known, the terror would not exist. In fact, we will argue here that the terror would not exist if it were known either way. Perhaps this is an overstep; is not knowing if you will be eaten by a bear better than knowing? Who can

say? Only one who has been both the escaped and the d
And they are in no condition to offer much of an opinion on the second encounter. But it is true that fear is the killer. Fear cannot be allowed to control us, or it will destroy us. Because, as with the hunter, fear grows to its own horrors. A sound that is unknown, if feared, will grow into an eldritch monstrosity and will continue to grow until it is faced and defeated. The hunter tracked his monster even though he didn't want to. He strongly desired to run away but was strengthened by love. The love of his son, people, and his community.

We will argue that fear is the feeling of the unknown. It is the experience of the void, where spiritual attainment is absent. Confronting the unknown gives us knowledge. So fear is as the emptiness of a vessel, and confronting the emptiness is the act of filling the vessel. Fear is not the presence of the unknown but the absence of the Love, as earlier defined as the thought of creation. And this is what we mean when saying that fear is good. Because fear is emptiness. Fear is the emptiness of the clay. Uncontrolled, it is terror and darkness. It is the horrors of our world and our nightmares. But controlled, it is the molded hollow that turns a lump of clay into a usable bowl for drawing water.

We leave our old world behind by the hand of the Avatar. Then, we use the waters that surround us and mix them into the remains of our world, the clay husk that remains. And with this clay, we create in it a hollow, and create a vessel, and can call it a bowl or a body. And with this body, we explore the new world and higher understandings of the Infinite. And this rise is begun by overcoming our fears. And this is done by knowledge. And where knowledge is wanting, by faith. God is the Unknown, and the Unknown can be called by the names fear, or faith. Faith is just old knowledge, smaller things that we knew before. We call this unknown by the name of God, reminding ourselves that this same unknown was there at the foundation of the universe and watched over the formation of the stars and planets. This unknown drew forth life from stone, and made of it worlds to thrive within. This same unknown is the bringer of life to this very moment and has been planned for a long time ahead. And this unknown is the Infinite Endless that thought to introduce itself to us by the small name of God so that we would look upwards to itself. And we can have faith that this endless draw will not end any time soon. We feel fear when we do not feel the love resonating from the unknown. To counter such fear, to master and control it, we need only to understand that we are always in the infinite mind of the creator. Or, to say it another way, we are not outside of the system; we are a part of it. In a third way, we are an instance of the Cascade of Causality, and we belong here.

And this was the strength of the hunter: that he used to face the bear. Love, love for his community and faith in his knowledge, in his skill, and in his Infinite Creator that has led him and his people for so long. His creator that has had him in mind since the dawn of creation, and his creator that has the whole world in his hands. It is from here that he derives his boldness. This is the strength of the hunter, and it can be ours as well.

15

Key and King

If there is one thing to understand, it is that we are not outside of the universe. We are not outside of the system. Our world is so very different from that that of nature; everything has and knows its place. Trees grow, predators hunt, and omnivores forage. All of these moving parts of the ecosystem flow in perfect harmony. And then there is us, humankind, bumbling around the planet, having no idea of our purpose, place, or function. In fact, coming to the conclusion that we have none. We exist as some kind of unfunny cosmic joke or misstep. As a bug in the system, a flaw in the design. God has given us no reason for why this Earth is spinning, why this galaxy is shining, or why we are here. He has given no answer, tangible or presentable, to our questions on these topics, leaving us in a desperate and often hopeless state as if we were some random occurrence that just so happened to fumble into consciousness. But maybe the reason for this is that of what we are, as some kind of "primordial soup," from which something better will crawl out. Perhaps what we are feeling is (to a greater degree) what the primordial goo that our life crawled out of some millions of years ago. Perhaps it, too, felt like this, purposeless, and wandering. Full of disorder, and yet having so much potential. Maybe it felt depressed as well, wondering what it could become, wondering if it had a future, and wondering if whatever cause created it, cared for it at all. Maybe it, too, was lonely.

But as we can see from our vantage point in this far future, what wonders did emerge. We wouldn't have dogs if it weren't for that goo. Ostriches, penguins, and water buffalo, each such a wonder to behold. Imagine seeing a chicken again for the first time. The fact that it exists is so amazing. And then imagine that feeling of seeing a chicken for the very first time, but from a mind that knows the extent of physics, astronomy, and the higher maths. Imagine being a mind that knows the probability of life evolving and the requirements of proteins to form. And seeing, from that mind, for the very first time, a chicken. And witnessing with these eyes all that has come about from the primordial soup that felt so alone, pointless, purposeless, depressed, and even afraid. Imagine if that goo had given up, let go of its desires for higher things, and melted down into the dust. Imagine if it chose not to form; imagine if it just laid, and died. From a place of knowing all that it could do and all that it could become if it only kept the faith. And of the beauty that exists because it didn't give up. Now imagine the future that will exist, if we don't give up either. The force that brings proteins together to form cells is the same force that brings us together to form communities. Because, in reality; this is nothing new. The same patterns repeating themselves at higher and higher frequencies and sizes. The forces of creation continually oscillating. And all that we feel is the feeling of evolution and momentum and growth. In fact, the study of God can be equated to the laws of thermodynamics. And in this way, God is thrust.

Earlier, we asked why God would insert himself into his own creation. Maybe it's because he doesn't and that there is a force of thrust in the universe. The "thought of creation" that flows from the Infinite Endless. And this force is the cause of all motion. It just flows through different lenses (worlds/perspectives), and through these lenses, it takes differing appearances. We just like to get attached to words, that is all. We feel like "God" is important, but we could call it "life" or "purpose" all the same. We could even call it "jive" or "whoosh." It really doesn't matter. We can call it by so many names, but what matters is that we recognize it. The problem arises when we separate the force that drives us from the force that unites us. Because there is only one force, and our drive should be our unity. There is only one God, and not two opposing. And this is the meaning of "God is love." It means that the force that creates us is not a force of division, or conquest, or power. It is not a force of fear or of hatred. That primordial soup chose love over fear, even though it didn't know that it had a future. Even though it didn't know that from all the darkness in the universe, it would invent (through cause and consequence) the most powerful of flashlights and lighthouses. And relationships that brighten the universe. Despite not knowing, it grew, and it didn't die; it chose love.

Maybe it's not that God is love. God is the thrust of our higher will; it is our combined intent. God is our purpose, and our manifest destiny. Maybe it isn't that God is love, but that love has to be our God, and also, that we can see God as our creator. through this lens, "God is love" means that through

... .he suffering and hardships that we have endured, all the wars, greed, and persecutions, it wasn't the hate or the fear that created us. God is our creation, our creator. And it was love that created us. Like the goo that came before us, we didn't grow from hate or lust for power; we, too, chose love. And thought yet another lens, God is everything, God is the Infinite. And it is not the darkness that we see when we look out into the universe; it is the light. And even when our night is dark, the universe is still ever filled with stars, standing for eons, just shining their light out into the endless universe. And the primordial goo grew and evolved by the intent of the universe. And so, too, can we. God is infinite, and God is love. And maybe that is the true meaning of God is love, that love is infinite.

Maybe "God is love" is small and personal. God is the purpose and the direction of your life. God is both your goal and your path. God is both life and life force. By "God is love," we mean that you should not act in fear or retaliation, not in destruction and building walls but in creation and building bridges. And this is a declaration of who we are and how we choose to see the world. We choose forgiveness and lifting each other. When we choose, as the goo before us, to build a better world. Even though it didn't know what beautiful life would come from its decision, maybe this is what it means to say "God is love." All lenses look to the same force. "God is love" is a choice, made by both the Primordial Singularity, and the primordial soup. And the primordial us, before the birth of a new world.

Perhaps of those reasons God never gave us, and the questions he answered with silence. Maybe the answer lies in what we have been given. In the same way as the left front tire in the car analogy from before. God has given us no reason for our existence and no answer to the questions of our existence. All he has given us is each other and the ability to care. He has given us a world to explore and a home to return to. A mind to ask questions and enough questions to overflow that mind. Maybe humanizing and anthropomorphizing God has backfired in some ways. Maybe we should look less for the creator and more for creation. Less of the beginning and more of the return. Suppose we're not supposed to be searching, because we have everything that we need. And suppose we're not supposed to be lost because we are exactly where we belong. Maybe we're supposed to be like those stars, that fill the universe, simply shining out our light, our grace, and our kindness. And what if we are? Can we see ourselves not for what we lack or what we think but for what we are? As we are? We've spoken about God and about love. And about what a world is, static perception without growth. And all of these ideas are from our perspective. And if we are like plants, growing up toward heaven, maybe we should try to see it from the perspective of the sun, as a small life, receiving of our light.

We have used a lot of words here: world, Avatar, endless, and God. We want to pause for a personal second to try to understand something very important before we continue. The wisdom is what exists before your eyes. You see it, you know it, you live it every day. The difference is a level of attainment or understanding of exactly what is going on in that life, lived every day. The concept introduced of "vernacular juggling" is the most important in this book. Because you probably have a grasp of every single concept in this book, but by a different name. We think so little of it because we don't see how it is as real as the physical world around us. We feel like it is only our perception and meaningless in the grand scheme of things. But it is not; the spiritual world is more real than anything we can touch, smell or see, even though it feels like it is just in your head. Because it is one step closer to reality. And we can prove this thought. First, to see (spiritually) is to understand. You can see the visible spectrum with your corporeal eyes. But you can "see" that the visible spectrum is only a small part of the true spectrum of light, and that sight is with your spiritual eyes. So you can see that your spiritual eyes see more of reality than your physical eyes. The purpose of defining our terms is not in the terms, but in the definitions. If, in the definition, you are reminded of a word or concept that goes by another name, remember our vernacular juggling and see an old world through new eyes. There is a lot of wisdom in old writings; they are just written in different languages and from different eyes. But truth is universal, and learning to see past the differences, learning to see from another's eyes, is the greatest skill that can be gained. It is the core of love over fear. It is key, and it is king.

IV

Life

16

Chapter Sixteen

On a blustery late afternoon, two days into a last-minuet business trip to some strange city. Walking back to your lodging, from a somewhat disappointing luncheon at a local pub. The chilly air has begun to cut through your overcoat and thin gloves as you softly curse yourself for not bringing a worthy headpiece. A small shop draws your eye, an obscure bookshop. And upon opening the door, your wishes are granted. The heat is on, and the air is toasty warm. The old shopkeeper has a faint look of hailing from a warmer climate. Directly into the shop, your feet fall on a short staircase as the shop sits in a half basement. It is cramped and cluttered. The dim lights are blocked by the tall shelves and piles of books. It begins as an excuse after a friendly nod to the old shopkeeper. She gives you a pleasant, but cautious greeting as you pretend to show interest in her wares. But as you meander through a few of her avenues, looking over her collection, a shadow draws your eye. In the deep, far corner, within a cubby hole made of a collapsed stack of larger books. It just resembles a cave, in a painting by younger eyes. And it draws you, not ecting to spend much more time in this store, as the feeling beginning to return to your nose and ears. But as you draw closer, bend down, and look within, a small book catches your eye. It is a little black book, more of a dark grey, that was surly black before. It is not much bigger than your hand and has a width that fits perfectly within your grasp. As you reach for it, and wrap your hand around its spine, it feels as if you have held this book before. It feels familiar, which is not surprising, really, as most books have a roughly similar feel to them. But as you retrieve this book, you see it has no title, either on the cover or on the spine. It has nothing upon it whatsoever. But as it is in your hand now, it just sparks your curiosity. You take it up to the counter and request a price from the little elder. She looks over the book with no recognition at all. She can find no code or identifying mark upon it. And has no record of an unmarked little black book at all. She says you can take it with you, free of charge.

But you offer to give her something for it, if not just in thanks for the warmth from the chilly day and for offering such a pleasant little shop to explore. You take the little book back out into the fierce weather, tucking it away into your coat and turning up the lapel against the winds. You continue on your way. But the walk is different; there is a palpable energy exuding from the book. Your mind holds onto it as if it were enticing you with some bewitching power.

By the time you return to your room, your curiosity has evolved. After hanging up your coat, you turn up the thermostat and put on the kettle. You place your new acquisition on the desk, wrap yourself in a blanket for added warmth, sip your beverage, and open the cover. And you are transported. There is no other term for it, no other language to describe it. You read of a young man taking sail, his first time away from home. He and three others traveling to a small town in northern Bolivia to work as missionaries. And with them, you sail the harsh seas. You travel over lands, in cars and on trains. You hike through the jungle and tend to your brother, who has injured his leg. And with your friends, you serve the small village for a time, and then you fall in love. You experience a crisis of faith and are torn between your duty to the church and the native beliefs of these people. Your new love draws you into yet another world. A world of oneness with the Earth. You take part in pagan rituals and tribal magic. You learn histories and stories and see the world in a whole new way. And on that night, love becomes lover.

You meet your friends in the morning, a twist of shame but not of remorse. You live two lives for a time, but in time your mission ends. You desire to stay, but you are not of this world. Your studies call, your plans for university. Your family expects you, and you have obligations to your church and kin. After all, they paid for your trip and lodging. Your three friends whisper relentlessly in your ear, and each one makes such good and valid arguments. You share a tearful goodbye with your love, as there will be no conversation about leaving. You have to leave and to do so alone. Your friends are strong for you as you journey back through the jungle. Your brother begins to fall ill on the train to the harbor and falls asleep on the ship. It is in black weather you sail home. With half your heart, you yearn to lay eyes on your mother. To greet your family and be welcome back into your church body. Your loving community. You cannot wait to begin courses at the university, and your future is all planned, bright as the morning sun. But half of your heart remains in Bolivia, and you wonder if you made the right call. You turn the last page, and close the back cover, look around your small room, and remember your present business. You tuck the book back into your belongings and prepare yourself for your meeting with some foreign investors. You look over your notes and spreadsheets, and everything seems to be in order. Your coworker bangs on your door, energized by the smell of money and the bathtub of coffee he has been drinking since you arrived. And you go with him and give your presentation. You talk when it is your time to talk. And you listen when it is your time to listen. It ends triumphantly, and you hurry back to your room. With rushed packing, you hurry to the airport, only releasing a massive sigh of relief when at the gate to your flight. Boarding is easy, and you sit in your window seat and look out at the runway. As the wheels begin to turn, and you watch the terminal grow farther away. You can't help but feel, as if half your heart was left in Bolivia, and you wonder if your friends were wrong to pull you away.

There is reading a book, and then there is the experience of reading a book. And they are vastly different things. But keep in mind that nothing in this universe is out of place. And nothing is without its connection to everything. Your mind is not a drifting void, separate and unconnected. The Spiritual Dimension is where your mind dwells. And it is a world just like any other. There is a reason that a book cover and a door swing the same way. They both take you from one place to another. The magic of a book is not an escape from reality; it is an escape to reality. Because the universe is not about the static facts and random logics. It is life, emotion, energy, and growth. You cannot study a car engine by just memorizing the pieces; they have to be together, and they they have to run. Just like you don't study a book by counting the number of letters and the words most repeated, you don't know a book by how much it weighs, the type of paper, or the brand of ink. Because the true book is purely spiritual. The paper you hold is only the portal to where it exists in the higher dimension.

Contrary to the beliefs of some, there is no talk about God, without talk about love, life, books, art, dancing, and the vast, limitless expanse of the stars in the sky. Each a sun of its own little worlds. Full of their own love, and life, and books, and art, and dancing. And each with their own limitless expanse of stars in their sky. Because this is God. God is the Universe. Do not lose sight of life, or you will surely be dead. A book on God is a book on everything, and thus, everything must be inside it. God is infinite and cannot be grasped or understood. But that isn't really true. Thought the mind cannot entrap him, the heart can experience his presence in all manners. It is in this example that the mind wants to drink while the heart wants to swim. But it is really difficult to do both at the same time. It takes a balance, drinking and swimming, drinking and swimming. But take care not to drink too much wine before swimming, and take care not to pee in the ocean.

We've delved into the cascade and the worlds that contain it; all that remains is the act of receiving it. But this is a complex conversation because the "it" is all, and the "receiving" is existence. The name of the lord is called unpronounceable because it is spoken with every breath. The study of the universe, science, is only done by separating a small bit of it for study. And whereas even a small bit of the universe does hold the "DNA" of the Infinite, that DNA is infinite in depth. Just as infinite in depth as the universe in scope. By this, we mean that there is a whole world below the atomic and worlds upon worlds beneath the subatomic that we cannot even fathom. A small object that you can hold in one hand, like a book, for example, contains more atoms than stars in the known universe, and each one of those atoms, if sized to that of the known universe, would not lay empty. And God is the creator of it all. That is all; Infinite is his only attribute. So seeking him, studying him, is not really seeking or studying him. It is just seeking; it is just studying. Living for God is not really living "for" God. It is just, "living." In what way can we assume that this God does not have us (our lives and stories) all planned out? This Infinite is the author, and we exist because (cause and effect) of him. And our infinite curiosity bears his signature. This is the mindset required for a true foray into the study of God.

17

The Great Work

There is no study of God; there is no Godology. The very idea is insane, as there is no study of the universe in its entirety without any separations or divisions. Because the study of God is what is being done, not in your world but in all the worlds above and beyond. While self-aware, it is what is still unaware. While reading, it is everything unread, and while looking it is everything unseen. Self-awareness is the beginning of the study as much as getting out of bed in the morning is the beginning of a marathon. It is merely one of a myriad of names used to call out into a vast emptiness and dark void. It is a state of mind, a state of spiritual growth, and it is called the work. In some circles, it is called the Great Work (some circles are more eccentric than others). The Great Work is the story of the Pilgrim. It is from the day he was born to the day that he dies. And even beyond. How he learns to return to the land of the living and how he makes his way to the King's castle and within. It is the story of how he makes his way to to the most sacred storehouses of the King and lays his hands on the most

,ures in the kingdom. It is how he finds his way to
 and takes his seat, realizing that he was the King
and that this is only the beginning of his story, not
Because then there is the story of the King, his battles
 ars, and where he goes, and what he does. It is how he
 declares war on the heavens and invades with his armies. It is
how he raises his armies and marches to the gates of heaven.
It is how he conquers the demons and casts down the angels.
Finding the throne of heaven empty and sits himself upon it,
finding that it was his thrown all along, and that he had just
found his way back to his home. But he is not home yet; he
has only found another story that needs to be told and a higher
heaven that needs to be won. This is the Great Work, and it is
the only work of value. It is from this work that it is said, "he
who does not work, shall not eat." Because to eat is to grow,
and the work, was earlier introduced, as "reaching up."

Pilgrim is the name of the state of being, or state of mind, of
growth. It was described as the act of using one's old worlds
to make bowls. And using these bowls to draw drinking water
from the ocean of the Infinite. This is a fancy way of saying,
to use your knowledge to scrape away at the unknown, and
accepting those shavings of reason into yourself as further
knowledge.

The previous example given of the Great Work, of conquering heaven and sitting on the throne, Is written in what can be called, a "language of branches" (like metaphor). You will not be physically slapping angels. So we will return to the Great Work later. First, we will discuss the work. (The difference is intensity.)

It was introduced earlier that the work is creating a bowl and splashing the ocean, and this is true, but here we will explain what that means. After all, it was also said earlier that "receiving is existing." The work is not existing; the work is the conscious effort of growing. The work was introduced as the state of Pilgrim. God makes the Pilgrim. When he introduces himself in the world as his Avatar, he draws you by the hand out of your world. Now, this does not mean that one must sit and wait. What this means is that what is happening is of God (the unknown) and is therefore not understood. What this means is that one does not have to understand what is happening or why.

You do not have to know how a meal gives you strength and energy for that meal to give you strength and energy. You do not have to understand how a plane flies to board it. God sends his Avatar to you and begins your journey to a holy place, thus making you a Pilgrim. Now, Pilgrim has been introduced as a state of self-awareness, but here we will go deeper. Self-awareness is being aware of your own perceptions and how things may not be the way you see them to be. But the Pilgrim is more than that. Because the Pilgrim is not just a person walking, but a person on a walk to a place. He knows where he is going (or has a place in mind, even though he has never been there). So self-awareness is only the beginning; one must also be aware of one's creator.

To be in this state, to be a Pilgrim, first think about your thinking. See yourself where you are, as you are. Be self-aware. Then realize that you are sitting in a universe, there are a multitude of stars around you, and galaxies upon galaxies, and all of this exists. Thirdly, remember that everything (including yourself) is within a vast system of cause and effect, with every object ricocheting off of every other object all of the time, cause and effect (including the mind and within your own mind).

Every cause must have its own cause, and every effect must have its own effect. Finally, there must be a cause of all causes, or a creator. We know nothing of this creator, only that it exists. And within all of creation, you exist. And that's it, the state of being aware of yourself, and of your creator. This is being a Pilgrim because in such a state, despite everything that one learns and in every way that one grows, one never loses sight of where they are going; they never lose sight of their destination. This state of being is a relationship with that creator, and this is because we anthropomorphize the system of cause and effect, saying that everything that cascades down from creation is the will (think physics) of the creator. And that even our state of wanting to know our creator is the will of the creator.

This is the Pilgrim (the awareness of the self), on his journey with the Avatar of the Infinite (the awareness of the creator). So what is the next step? This is not a hypothetical journey within our imagination; it is what we are physically doing right now. It was introduced earlier that you are your self-aware consciousness. You are the Pilgrim, and God is the Infinite, the universe (everything outside of you), or the ocean. And you are swimming and drinking. Living and learning. They are two different states, while growth exists in between them. And this is where we introduce the bowls, for without the bowls, we are swimming, and with the bowls, we are splashing. Without the bowls, we are drinking ocean water, but with the bowls, we are drawing pure water to drink. And what is a bowl? A bowl is the self-awareness of a past world. It is skill, expertise, mastery, and art. And it is anything; it can be a musical instrument, or a physical tool, or even a specific field of education. It is the self-awareness of a skill, expertise, mastery, or art. The work is the creation of bowls. And the Great Work is using those bowls to attain higher and even higher understandings of your creator.

And so there is no study of God because God is the all, and the "study" is is existence. The name of the lord is called unpronounceable because it is spoken with every breath. And every leaf is as infinite in depth as the universe is in scale. There are worlds below the subatomic and above the known universe. Seeking him is not seeking "him." It is just seeking. Studying him is not studying "him," it's just studying. Living for him is not living for "him;" it's just living. Seeking, studying, and living, but all in the awareness of the self and of the creator. Seeking, studying, and living, as a Pilgrim on a journey to a sacred place. This is the mindset required for a the study of God.

18

The Pilgrim's Path

To the reader, this book probably seems theist in nature, even though previous chapters may have stated positions that seem odd or contrary. The overall tone and constant use of the word "God probably led you to believe that this is at least some kind of deist text. This book is not meant to be aloof, imprecise, or vague. So, let us be completely clear in our opinions of this: Atheism is wrong because God undoubtedly exists, and his presence is clear. Atheism is right because God is totally made up, and opinions about him have no grip on reality. What can we possibly mean by this? Let's dig into it.

Your God is your understanding of the Infinite, being neither understanding nor infinite. What this means is that your god is the expanding of your consciousness. But it is not "you," "expansion," or "consciousness." And here is the difference between your God (my god/our god) and God himself. We have zero attainment in God himself because God is infinite, and God is the Infinite (same thing). "Your God" is not even the tip of his toenail. And to conflate the two is blasphemy because understanding is understanding. And a name is (as discussed earlier) a level of understanding. So, to say "My God" is the same as God himself is to say that I understand Infinity and have it firmly grasped in my hand. So, blasphemy. But blasphemy does not hurt God, just us. In this state, one cannot grow, one cannot learn or be taught, and one is in a state lower and worse than death.

This is not to say that God and "My God" are different beings. Our God is our journey toward God himself, the growth of our understanding. Even though this concept was discussed earlier, we will discuss it again. The use of the word "himself" denotes the nature and anthropomorphization of causality; it is not a declaration of God as a dude in a white robe.

There is a modern way to explain the spiritual aspect of the study of God and even the Spiritual Dimension itself. And this may aid the understanding of the previous two statements on atheism. This example would be the common pastime, video games. Everything in a virtual world had to be programmed and written in a coding language. If you press a button, and the little character jumps on the screen, every aspect of this has to be programmed and written in code. If you discover a secret location, you do not say to yourself, "Oh my, did the developers know?" They did know because it, too, had to be programmed and written in code. So, too, does your mind exist. Visualize a huge bank and skulk down to the lower basement and into a massive vault. Lock the door behind you and enter into a super secure, deep, deep second vault. And lock yourself in that one as well. And here in this secret place, you think about a pink chihuahua. Do not think to yourself, "Oh my, I am completely disconnected from the system of existence." Do not think to yourself, "Oh my, can "God" know of this?" You are not disconnected, and "God" does know of it. To use "developer speak," the vault exists in a file, as does the super-secret vault, and it is only shown on the screen by accessing said file. And you would have to access the "dogs in color" folder to get the pink chihuahua. If you could see it from the programming language, you would see no secrecy at all. A "secret area" is not a secret in the code; only in the game. Your mind is a part of the world; it only feels separate because you are unaware of the connections. God is the developer, you are in the game, and your God is your understanding of the code. And this is because the developer wrote the code from his heart. And you can get to know the developer through his art. The word God is just a name, a level of understanding of the creator (humanized cause) of existence.

Your God is your (personal and within your own perspective) understanding of the Infinite. And if the name of your God does not change with the passing of days, then you are lost. Because God is love, and love is creation, if one were to say that they are a receiver of this love of God and are not growing in love and understanding, then there has been some miscommunication as they are not who they say they are. This is a very serious issue because this is what it means: "Depart from me, I never knew you." If you pray using the same name as you did as a child, you may as well use your name instead. Because the God you pray to is not God but your own understanding. It is not your understanding of the Infinite because you have lost sight of the Infinite, and it is just your understanding. This is what is meant by "Their gods are their own stomachs." Now, this is not something to be scared about, just something to be aware of. If you are aware of it, then you are undoubtedly on the right path. This is because this awareness is a state of mind that is both self-aware and aware of the creator. Being aware of the creator is being aware of the Infinite and the Endless. This awareness is a state of mind and a state of growth. You may not be growing as fast as others, or you may be growing faster but with weaker roots. It's not a race; it's a journey to an ever closer relationship with an infinite entity, being all that exists. This state of mind is often called the Kingdom of God. This is what is meant: "Seek first the kingdom of God, and lean not on your own understanding." This is not about the mastery of life because life is not a thing that can be mastered. And when we believe otherwise, it is because we have lost sight of our creator. And this is the balance, awareness of the self, and awareness of the creator. Most issues in our growth can be attributed to one or the other.

A small question will be discussed here: if all of this is true, then why did God create a world with other people in it? It seems thus far in this book that it is all about God, and You. Where do the others come into it? We divided everything earlier between the God and the You. But the You is not your toes or your body; it is your knowledge and your consciousness. Everything outside of the You is the God (or the Unknown). And the God (Unknown) is as a friend and sojourner. So, as it was hinted at earlier, the consciousness of the others is not so separate from the consciousness of the You. Other people exist (of course), but we have to separate the other people from our perception of the other people. There is the person as they stand in our perception, and there is the person as they are, from their own perception. And it is only when we try to see them as they really are that they are with us. If we only care about our perception of them, then it is as if they are not there. Because we are so entrenched within our own world, there is no place for them to reach out to us. We can see this as loving one another, not using them for our own benefit, but seeing the soul inside them and seeing them as their own You (self or conscious entity). Building those connections expands our consciousness. Building community is growing closer to God, our creator, because we love the others that he gave us to love, and in so doing, we are breaking our old worlds and perceptions.

And this is an important part of the study of God. So much so that the sages (old dudes who wrote books) have said that there is no study without a group. Only with a group of sojourners are we able to practice the expansion of consciousness (recognition of the souls of others) that we learn about by studying the creator (of love itself). Loving one another is the same as seeing through each other's eyes. This is what it means that it is key because it expands our consciousness and allows us to learn many more of the names of God.

19

A Touch of Necromancy

There is another term for the awareness of the Pilgrim or of the work itself. And that is life, or being alive. We understand this term quite well when talking about our interests or hobbies. Being alive is activity, joy, and passion. It is that vivacious, tingly energy of truly enjoying yourself with your activities. We often use this term of being alive, and we can understand how this is a spiritual life that comes from spiritual fulfillment. In earlier chapters, warnings of different concepts or ideas that could cause death have been mentioned. Here, it will be described and defined because death is the opposite state of spiritual life. Even though it is not as final as physical death, it should be understood and avoided in the same way.

Death is when your life ends, when your growth ends. When you are no longer vibrant and alive. It is quite comparable to physical death. As the purpose of the soul is to grow in the love of God; when we are spiritually dead, we are simply not growing. In the study, it is when you are no longer interested. You stop caring. You stop fighting, stop trying, stop studying, doesn't matter to you anymore. Now, this can ...inful, especially if you insert your own enjoyment and ...ies. You can feel what it would be like to no longer gain pleasure from those activities and how it would feel as if a part of you did die. But just like in the flesh, it is only when you are alive that there is any fear of death or any struggle in the dying. This is because once you are dead, it is as if you were never really alive at all; you remember caring but cannot recall why. You won't remember what it was to be alive, or how it felt. Life will just be a thing that you once had, and you cannot remember why it was important to you. It was just the "past" you. Those actions just don't spark any interest in you anymore. And as you can see, this is not a bad thing. To be spiritually dead is just as common and natural as normal physical death. To spiritually die is to not care anymore, and in one way, it should not scare you. Because you merely do not care. But in another way, it is worse than dying in the flesh. Because the time will pass in a blur, and you will wake up old. And you will wake up empty. To die in the spirit is not for life, but it can be for a while. And a life unlived is a terrifying reality to wake up to.

So take care when a text warns you that "you will surely die," because what it is referring to is not your heart spontaneously exploding but your passion fizzling out. You lose interest and walk away, maybe even never to return. It is written that one cannot truly study the wisdom of God without a group. And this is because passion fuels passion. The study can be done alone, but life is never really life, and in death, one is unaware of one's state. It is like learning a great deal about a location and then just never going there. It is only with a group that life truly comes alive, and death actually stands opposed.

You can imagine this as if you were in a group of around

ten and studying a vast and interesting topic. You are all so deeply invested in this study. But one day, one of your friends is absent and not feeling it today. This is not bad; it is like they are asleep. We all sleep and need a break now and again. But if a friend were to lose interest altogether, we can see how to the group it is as if he were dead. Dead to the group as in dead to the study. Not dead to you as a person; you still talk and could even share other activities. It is just that they have lost all interest in the work that you and the group are doing. And this is death. Felt more deeply in a group, than on one's own. Alone, one cannot truly tell if they are alive or dead, as corporeality requires some participation from another. So this is death, and we can see that death is not bad, but it is a state that one would rather avoid if possible. One's study should be in life and in sleep, and to die is a deep sadness. But this is spiritual death, and spiritual death can result in spiritual reincarnation. Your friend can return and come back to the group with a new life, a new perception, and a desire for the study.

There is a natural order of life and death. And in this way, death and sleep can be seen in the same spectrum. One is merely deeper and may be permanent. And if they do return, they return with a different desire and a different understanding. This is natural in any study, but especially in the study of God. Because with wisdom comes knowledge, and the knowledge of this life and death. And it is important to be very careful not to dabble in necromancy. If a friend dies in the work, it is important to let them rest in peace and not to try and reanimate them. Returning their soul is something that only God can do. You can reanimate them, but this will not be new life; it will not be life at all. They are not alive, and you are not allowing them to die. So, they are not resting and cannot reincarnate.

Even if you let go and let them pass on, your actions will have poisoned them, and their soul may not find its way back. So do not dabble in necromancy, and let them rest in peace.

Death in the spiritual is not the end. If you die (spiritually) of natural causes, your soul (Pilgrim) will reincarnate (spiritually) in a new body (desire, bowl/vessel, again spiritually, think penguin in a top hat). And your journey will recommence. But there are many other ways to die. You cannot over extend yourself to the extent that your body (desire) dies, but your mind (reason) does not. You become like a zombie, with no life in your studies and no life in the work, but you still shamble on. This is bad for your group because if you "bite" them, they will lose their life as well. If they sleep, they will die but will be unable to die naturally and will become a zombie like you. And your entire group can die this way, studying without life or passion. And as we know, the only way to kill a zombie (because they have no life in their body) is to pierce the brain. To use logic and reason to convince your friend that they have lost all passion and need to rest. There are many other diseases that your spiritual body can contract. And each one must be cured in their own way. If a friend becomes vampiric (they gain their life desire for study by siphoning from others (taking, not sharing)), even death is not the end of their condition. Only by a stake of wood piercing their heart can they finally die. Remember the viscosity of thought, and you can find wood. Pierce their heart, and they will find rest and may safely reincarnate. But be warned because a "bite" from a vampire turns you into a ghoul, which is just a step up from a zombie. There is still some life left, but all passion will be drained away. In such a state, you will find no pleasure in your studies.

Now, these states and amalgamations of spiritual death mixed with fear and anger, are explained here in order to help one read old texts with new eyes. We mentioned the "branches" language earlier, where every spiritual thing is given a corporeal root in order to discuss these unseeable things with others. However, this language is also used to expound on the word mentioned before, which is called blasphemy.

Because blasphemy is not life or death; it is a state beyond either. Life is considered spiritual growth, so one who commits blasphemy is not dead because they, indeed still grow larger. But their growth is not from the love of God. They grow on a tincture of fear, pride, and greed. It is like a snake bite, where just a small amount of venom enters, and the area begins to expand on its own, with a vile, thick puss. This is what blasphemy does to the blasphemer. Their body and desire grow from within with the creation of a selfish bile and a hateful and conceited sick. In this state, no love can enter them, and no physician can help. They are toxic to themselves and others. But they cannot see this because they have lost sight of both their creator and themselves. And so they grow and expand from their own fetid arrogance, thinking all the while that they are alive, but they do not feel alive.

They are neither dead nor undead. They are not reanimated, zombie, or ghoul. Alone, there is no hope because they cannot even perceive their own state, and nothing can reach into their worlds to help them. The only end to this state is death. But they cannot die because the venom and bile within them cannot die, as it is not alive. The only way to stop this existence is to tear out their heart and burn it in fire. Only then will the body die. But the scars of blasphemy are not only on the body but the soul itself. This means that when the soul reincarnates, it will be scarred deeply, and its next life must be devoted to healing others. This next life cannot grow; its purpose is found only in the service of others. If it does not do so, then the scars will remain for incarnation upon incarnation, and nothing can remove them. But the scars of blasphemy will whisper in the ears of this new body, and this whisper is as the venom before it. It can grow into new blasphemy. And sometimes, if a friend has succumbed to blaspheme, they must be cut off from the group. Because in the operation of saving their soul, you may very well lose your own. And a final note here: be very careful when separating the text of the spiritual world from the physical world. Do not, on any occasion, physically rip out your friend's heart and burn it with fire. That is murder and is a horrible thing to do. To "rip out their heart" spiritually is to show them, bluntly and with no flattery, that their current state is destroying their cause and a betrayal of their deepest held beliefs. And that they are hurting their friends. And if their soul is still present, they will see that they are hurting you and are blind to their growth and their journey. They will repent and put themselves to death (spiritually), cutting themselves off from their studies because they see that in their current state, they cannot see God.

see with spiritual eyes, and then they show us such magnificent sights. And there was no lie, from the first word to the last. But the eyes of others have been so sealed and so shut. Shut by the violence and darkness of the worlds around them. They do not see, and they cannot see. How can one tell them what wonders there are to behold, there, just past the veil of our broken, dying world? What waters could we pour on the wounded hearts?

The light cannot be hidden or covered, and the description of the physical does not give the truth justice. Because the truth is in the spirit, all the wonders to behold are in the spirit, and all the amazing things waiting are in the spirit. And where we may know that the spirit is the same as the mind, we may feel as if the spirit is distant, in some faraway land. Not for us and not in this life. Fantastical, whimsical, and otherworldly. So it may be. But where is the error in this? Whose idea was it that life should be without color or passion? From where did this boring existence of paperwork and daily commutes emerge? The reality is that we are standing in the middle of a massive universe full of wonder and beauty and darkness and burning balls of boiling plasma. And nowhere does it say that life should be paperwork and daily commutes. Life should contain passion, wonder, and screaming our truths from the tops of mountains or hills. Or the tops of tall buildings. This is life, nothing less.

This is life and not a word exaggerated. All that can be said of a good book is, "I was there." It is the same with God, "I was there." And it is the same with life. But to say it is the same with God is redundant because it is in fact, the same as God. Our art, our passion, our love, and our beauty are all a part of the cascade of the Infinite. We are all a part of the cascade because of who he is. We create because of what created, and was created, in us. We worship because of his order, and we revel because of his chaos. We write, and we sing, and we create. We love, because he first loved us.

God's relationship with us is the cause of our relationship with him and with each other. It is the Infinite cascade that waters us as seeds for infinite growth and desire. And that growth is the growth of our consciousness, understanding, and awareness. It is our awareness of others and our love for others. Our personal growth with God is tied to our relationship with others because together, we grow with God even further.

And when it says, "What you do unto the least of these, you do unto me," it is because everything that is outside of your world is the Infinite Endless, and everything you put out into the world is given to him, as an opportunity to give something to the one who has given us love and the cascade from the beginning. This is how God can be hungry and homeless. Cold and naked. A foreigner or an alien. A widow or a frightened child. It is an offering and an opportunity that he is giving us when he says "What you do to the least of these, you do to me." It is a celebration of love, both unto each other and unto God, when these words are said. It is a part of God's love that he gives us opportunities to love as he does.

Our lives and our experiences, our work both great and regular. Our path and our desire to resurrect that same feeling in others. This is not a side story of our existence; it is not a thing we should try to do on the weekends. Living, breathing, art, and dancing are our core and highest calling. To know God, and to love God, and to be in his presence. But God is infinite and is the Infinite, so can it not be said, to know, to love, and to be present? And he surrounds us, as each other, so that we can embrace him and feel his embrace. Life is the passion in our personal walks, our groups, and our studies. Our arts and our poetries and our songs and our dances. And our communities and our people. And this is what it means that God will grant us eternal life, not just a spiritual life, but the eternal life of those that we love when we love our peoples and our communities. And our dances and our songs, and our poetries. And our arts, our studies, and our groups. And when we love our own personal journeys, and our passions, and our God.

V

Conclusion

21

New Eyes

A lot of the ideas in this book are probably somewhat foreign to readers, and this is because of the language in which most books on this topic are written, not in a foreign language like in Greek or Arabic, but in a different kind of language altogether. These books are written in a spiritual language, a language of the mind and thinking parts. And the books speak only of this same dimension. Sadly, this is what happens when a bunch of people sit together in a room for too long and don't get out much. But this is also the only way in which precise and specific ideas are formed. So much so that if you're not in the in-group, you're not in on the lingo. And because there was a lot of stabbing and burning and crucifying going on, getting in on the in-group was kind of difficult. And this is one of those controversial topics tiptoed around in this text. Persecution is part and parcel of history and the study of God. This is why it is so important to be able to "quantum leap" into other people's lives and perspectives. To be able to feel as they feel, and love as they love. And to begin to heal the soul.

Growth is an infinite process, so this section is not serious or important. It is an attempt to exercise and open our new eyes, to see in new ways, and to read in new ways. Ideas, not edicts, which is why some frothy idioms are thrown in:

A few verses:

Numbers 23:19 "God is not man, that he should lie, or a son of man, that he should change his mind. Has he said, and will he not do it? Or has he spoken, and will he not fulfill it?"

This is in a spiritual (language) way; a man (spiritually) is a desire, an idea, and a complete thought. How we think and define the thoughts we think are not the same; this is kind of like the thought lying. And the son of a man is a natural conclusion, following idea, as in cause and effect. In this way, the son of a man often has a change of mind; otherwise, it would not be his son, just him. God does not lie in this way or change in this way. He is simplicity, singular, and unchanging. God "speaking" is a cascade, the cause and effect of the universe. If a boulder starts rolling down a hill, it is going to continue, and you had better not be on its path. Physics, and the laws of the universe are uncompromising. This does not take away from God being both infinite or personal; we need to make sure we are not using the word "just" to diminish reality.

James 1:5 "If any of you lacks wisdom, you should ask God, who gives generously to all without finding fault, and it will be given to you."

To ask is like to seek or look (the intent). If you lack knowledge, delve into the unknown; if you lack wisdom, delve into the Unknown. The words "generously" and "fault" may

2 Chronicles 7:14 "If my people, who are called by My name, will humble themselves, and pray and seek My face, and turn from their wicked ways, then I will hear from heaven, and will forgive their sin and heal their land."

"Called by my name" may refer to the level of understanding attained. The "my people" is what we call here in this book "Pilgrims." Remember when we held our hands out before our faces with one above the other? A metaphor for how God cannot be brought down. The only way is for us to rise. Well, rising has to be done consciously and requires help from above (or knowledge from the unknown). To study anything, you cannot think you know everything. This is humility. Turning from wicked ways is like learning and not bragging. And seeing his face is the point where learning becomes knowing. Heaven is where unknown knowledge is before it is known. Forgiving sins and healing land are the same things because of the viscosity of thought, land is fact.

Psalms 50:10 "For every beast of the forest is Mine, the cattle on a thousand hills. I know all the birds of the mountains, and the wild beasts of the field are Mine."

Every word is in the spiritual language, life is desire, and the viscosity of thought makes the land, water and air. Forests and fields are in realms of the mind, but this requires a more articulate teacher. This verse is included here to give a glimpse at what we are looking for in these old books and what we can glean. This is the oneness of God and how even the thoughts in our minds, the little fluttering ones, like birds, are not unknown to him. Even further, they are his. We only see his creation and explore his world.

have specific linguistic meanings to be studied but if one "asks" honestly, God is most generous, and answers will be given.

Deuteronomy 7:9 "Therefore know that the Lord your God, He is God, the faithful God who keeps covenant and mercy for a thousand generations with those who love Him and keep his commandments."

The name lord is the unpronounceable name and is the name referred to in this text as Avatar. This is a reminder to the fact that God and "My God" need to be the same, or I am just seeking "My" and nothing else because the "God" part does not move if I change focus. This focus is loving him and keeping his commandments. And his mercy is how he leads us "by the hand." His faithfulness is dependability, and for generations, he is referring to spiritual lives and deaths. As we grow and change in our attainment and understanding, he remains the same Infinite God.

1 John 4:7 "Beloved, let us love one another, for love is from God; and whoever loves has been born of God and knows God."

In the spiritual language, love is tantamount to the bestowal of thought or of positive focus. And the names of God here are Infinite and Wisdom. To know God is of closeness, and is talking about a person who is in the state of a Pilgrim. Being born of God refers to a second life (spiritual generations) of living for bestowal and not for the self. It may be controversial, but we want to use our vernacular juggling on that last part of this verse; it is not that one is righteous who follows the correct ideas, dots the right I's, and crosses the right T's. It says quite clearly here, that those who chose love over fear are righteous, even if they are not perfect in our eyes.

Ephesians 4:6 "One God and Father of all, who is above all, and through all, and in you all."

A singular creation by a singular creator. Infinite and Inevitable. Creation, the love that grows the creation, and the pull that draws the creation back to the creator. A major theme in the old books, said in more ways than one can count. But an important word here is "All." Father of all, and within you all. It is fear that divides us, but this Father is greater than fear. Maybe that is the purpose of this verse: unity, and unity through faith.

Genesis 1:1 "In the beginning, God created the heavens and the earth."

This is spiritual, but it is also physical and universal. There is a repetition of this concept. Creation is continual, but this verse is talking about the beginning of the personal journey or pilgrimage. Heaven and Earth both refer to the unknown and knowledge and the "body" and "mind" of the spiritual person. The body is your knowledge, and the mind is your focus on your studies. These two entities are created and work together, which is the story of Genesis.

Revelation 22:13 "I am the Alpha and the Omega, Beginning and End, the First and the Last."

Maybe this is referring to God by all names. Remember that while this is referring to God, the Infinite and Endless Cause of all Causes, it is being written by a human who is desperately trying to understand something without degrading it with his understanding. And there is a lot to understand. It looks like saying the same thing three times, but they are different. Alpha and Omega are Adoni and Endless, beginning and end are Avatar and Anthropomorphic, and first and last are Cascadence and Inevitable. But the point of this verse is to remember not to lower God down to us but to raise our minds upward, reaching up to him.

And a few sayings:

God is our refuge and strength.

Said by those who study God, to those who study God, as an explorer may find refuge and strength in the wilderness. It is home, where they belong. The unknown is the ultimate wilderness and grounds for exploration, and one can find their very definition inside of its depths.

As God is my witness.

This may be referring to the name of God described here as Inevitable, the cause-and-effect nature of the universe that was created in the beginning and is purely cascading out. Justice will be served not by moral hands but by the nature of the universe. Or maybe it is referring to the Infinite, as in, all is known in the infinite mind of reality, even that which was done in the heart, like intent.

All things are possible with God.

God as unknown, who armed us with a little knowledge to scrape away at his endless girth of unnameable things. Somewhere in there lie the answers to all questions, even the questions we have not thought to ask. But also God as Avatar, where we are capable of great things, even anything, if we set our minds to it. Only God knows how far we can go.

God works in mysterious ways.

The name is not Unknown, but Anthropomorphic; it is us wrestling with fitting the universe into our understanding of ourselves, along with maintaining hope in a better future in dark times. As discussed with the bear in the woods, say God, not unknown, to remind yourself that there is a system at work here, even if we don't understand it. It also doesn't hurt, and worrying can cause even more suffering than injury. Not always, but what else can be done? We must always press onwards, the choice is will it be in fear or in love?

An act of God

This idiom could be referring to God by any name, from Infinite, as in universal intent, to Inevitable of cause and effect, from a humanized deity to a personal touch from above. It can be anything, but it is a reminder, and that is important. We need constant reminders to "keep our eyes open," as it were. Until the state of being a Pilgrim is natural, it is an unnatural state. And it is easy to slip out of. Retaining awareness of yourself and your God can be strenuous. Some use mantras, some use jewelry, some get spiffy tattoos. Whatever will help remind you that you are alive, and keep you from falling asleep or, worse, dying. Because then, all that can wake you, is an act of God.

But for the grace of God

Grace is a loaded word, with tons of history and tomes written to its topic. But here we can adopt the non-holy definition of grace, as a simple elegance and the presence of God. The most ambiguous definition of God is just that feeling of being in the presence of some feeling of some heavenly substance. At some point, a relationship with God has to be purely personal, needing no reason or explanation. Usually, when this phrase is used it is after the closest shave of something quite detrimental, and you need a deep breath. And in that breath, you feel the grace of God.

Fear of God

What can be said about the fear of God? After all, God is love, God is light, and in him there is no darkness. Fear is separation, so how can we be afraid of that which is love and light? We could be afraid of failing him, but he is infinite, meaning that not only did he know of our failures, but he invented them. Far be it from us to know his mind. If he caused us to fail to do what we think he wants, maybe that says more about us than it does about him. Maybe there is another way to understand these three words. Fear of God, meaning to be afraid of God. Or fear of God, meaning God's fear. A good fear, a corrected fear. And what could that be if God creates, grows his creation, and then draws his creation back to himself? Maybe a good fear, is the fear that we are out of tune with his love. Fear that we are not living in his presence and in the proper state of mind. Fear of not being in a state, that we referred to here as Pilgrim.

22

The Gospel

The section layout of this book is probably recognizable to anyone reading it. They hold to the most common and copied verse of any book ever written. The simple Gospel, that any good witness to the grace and mercy of God will hold memorized. Certain things have been alluded to in this book because they are too controversial to face directly. But any true follower of any true God must strive with the same passion of their very life to tell others. There has been an attempt here to explain this, as only together can we rise higher in our understanding of God. But also, what has been attempted (and alluded to) here to explain is the difference between My God, and the Infinite. My God is my understanding, just as your God is yours. My God is from my perspective, just as your God is from yours. And when we seek the "MY" in my god, this divides us from each other. It is only when we seek the "God" in my god, that we are pulled by "his grace" together. The analogy of worlds was used to implore others to understand two things. One is that when we break out of our own worlds and our own perspectives, we do not break into reality. Reality is as infinite as God, and is God. But when we all break out of our own worlds and our own perspectives, the world we break into is one world. World peace is possible because the only thing separating us is our perspectives. And the only thing in our way is fear. Fear that our pain will hurt others, and fear that our trauma will infect others, blocking their eyes to the beauty around them as it has done ours. And if one thing can be declared with this text, it is that fear is not the presence of the unknown; it is the absence of love. We do not follow many gods, and this is why the many books repeat, and repeat and repeat. There is one God. One way, one truth, and one light. There is one future. There is one love. And the only thing separating us from oneness is our scarred and trauma-laden worlds. And this is why, repeated, and repeated, and repeated again. Is the Gospel. The purpose of this book is merely to reiterate it one more time:

For God so loved the world that he gave his only begotten son, that whosoever believes in him will not perish but have eternal life.

For God: The Infinite Endless, cause of all causes, unknown and unnameable, save for his infinitude and endlessness. But the specific name here is the name referred to in this text as Anthropomorphic. This is a name of God that is attainable, it is just outside our grasp without a little push.

So Loved: Cascadence, cause and effect, "so willed or so decreed" as gravity and quantum entanglement, not of hope but of scientific assurance as equal a part of this universe as matter itself, and as existence itself. As dependable as your reliance on your own consciousness.

The World: The seed. The egg that surrounds the infant child. The You, and your perspective. Knowledge and understanding. The growing plant (analogous) of your conscious being.

That He: The name here refers to the name above Infinite Endless, Ein Sof, is his name. it means the same thing: it is only in our minds that we want to make the distinction, Ein Sof is what exists before the Big Bang, before the infinite cascade. It is not separate; it is (to anthropomorphize it as well) like the separation between your consciousness and your thoughts. above his cascade of love, is his will.

Gave: Caused, created, by the will of the infinite. Cause and effect, as an effect of the love with which he created (emanated) the universe.

His only Begotten Son: The old English word "begotten" is kept and included because it means "fathered," as if to rule out adoption, or taking in. We briefly poked at this "language of branches," but it is quite detailed. Father and son are directly linked by cause and effect. God giving this son is not as a choice but a direct effect of the existence of God, known as the "thought of creation." The son of the unknown is knowledge. And the son of God is called Christ. Christ is an old word, which is worthy of a great deal of research in its own right. But in the same way as God is unknown, Christ is knowledge.

That Whosoever: Thus far we are talking about a universal constant. God creates, he grows his creation, and he draws his creation back to himself, and these three functions are the same. Growing his creation, is creation; drawing his creation is creation. Creation is growing his creation; drawing his creation is growing his creation. Creation is drawing his creation; and growing his creation is drawing his creation. Who is being created, grown, or drawn is irrelevant because all are being created, grown, and drawn.

Believes: This is the state of mind, this is the Pilgrim, and the Pilgrim is on his pilgrimage; it is who and what he is; it is in his name. If he wasn't on his pilgrimage, he would be dead, and he is not dead because he is Pilgrim.

In him: God by any name, from Adoni to Ein Sof, any understanding or attainment of reality whatsoever, no matter how small. Any Pilgrim, on any part of the road, is being discussed here. If he has only just begun, or is halfway there, this is creation, growing of the creation and drawing it back to himself.

Shall not Die: Death is the absence of growth. Death is the loss of faith. The loss of passion, desire, and life. Death is stillness, emptiness, and nothingness. And it, too, is a state of mind, and of being.

But Have: This is the dichotomy, the two ways. Vernacular juggling, pilgrim is not the state you have to be in to grow, and death is not the punishment if you are not toeing the line.
t you are doing when you are vibrant and alive,
f the Pilgrim, and if you are not living, you are

Everlasting Life: this is the Creator, drawing his creation back to himself. The third act in the one act of creation. Maybe it lines up with the universe expanding and shrinking. Perhaps it only appears this way. Who knows? The life of the universe or the life of one entity within the universe are equally sized to Infinity, and it is the Infinite that draws us to grow in knowledge and attainment. And equally in love and in community. One and the same.

"Ein Sof" means "without end." The name of God above Infinite Endless is Without End. And with a little vernacular juggling we can somewhat see what this means. If we think infinite and endless, we create a spiritual object with the parameters of infinite and endless. So the words "infinite" and "endless" don't mean infinite or endless, but the words without end do. When we think "without end," we don't think of anything. We create a "spiritual object" of a place where something is not there. And this is the closest we can come to understanding what God really is. We hold true to this one God even though we do not know who he is. Because of his many names, one is Hope. Hope in what we do know, and hope in each other. The Gospel recreates the initial act of God within us. It creates and recreates in us a desire. It feeds the desire and helps it grow. And it draws us towards the force of creation. The next name and the next level of understanding of God. This name is Divinity. And the Gospel is the way toward her.

We will try to end where we began, with a man named Adam, sitting on a stump and thinking about a better world. Around six thousand years ago, a man had an idea of a united world. And that idea has fought, and fought, and survived to this day. It is like a symbol, a banner, held above armies. Even though one can be torn, shredded, and burned. And even though it can be hastily drawn, some of the details missed. The symbol never dies and the banner is never destroyed. And its meaning never fades. No matter how much fear throws at it. And no matter what is faced. But the banner marches on, and what fear has divided, it can unite.

But at the end of the day, this is just ink on pages held in your hand, with no power and no magic. Its content is just a smattering of ideas, thoughts, dreams, and opinions of a bunch of people over a couple of years. Mere ideas. And it all can be condensed into these few simple lines:

Hell is very real, because hell is a world where we don't love each other. And God is very real, because God is a world where we do. So love the lord your God, with all your heart, soul, and mind. And love your neighbor as yourself.

Made in the USA
Coppell, TX
23 October 2025